Oriental Rambles

Also from Westphalia Press

westphaliapress.org

The Idea of the Digital University

Bulwarks Against Poverty in America

Treasures of London

Avate Garde Politician

L'Enfant and the Freemasons

Baronial Bedrooms

Making Trouble for Muslims

Philippine Masonic Directory ~ 1918

Paddle Your Own Canoe

Opportunity and Horatio Alger

Careers in the Face of Challenge

Bookplates of the Kings

The Boy Chums Cruising in Florida Waters

Freemasonry in Old Buffalo

Original Cables from the Pearl Harbor Attack

Social Satire and the Modern Novel

The Essence of Harvard

The Genius of Freemasonry

A Definitive Commentary on Bookplates

James Martineau and Rebuilding Theology

No Bird Lacks Feathers

Gems of Song for the Eastern Star

Crime 3.0

Anti-Masonry and the Murder of Morgan

Understanding Art

Spies I Knew

Lodge "Himalayan Brotherhood" No. 459 C.E.

Ancient Masonic Mysteries

Collecting Old Books

Masonic Secret Signs and Passwords

Death Valley in '49

Lariats and Lassos

Mr. Garfield of Ohio

The Wisdom of Thomas Starr King

The French Foreign Legion

War in Syria

Naturism Comes to the United States

New Sources on Women and Freemasonry

Designing, Adapting, Strategizing in Online Education

Gunboat and Gun-runner

Meeting Minutes of Naval Lodge No. 4 F.A.A.M ~ 1812 & 1813

Oriental Rambles

by George W. Caldwell, M.D.

WESTPHALIA PRESS
An imprint of Policy Studies Organization

Oriental Rambles
All Rights Reserved © 2014 by Policy Studies Organization

Westphalia Press
An imprint of Policy Studies Organization
1527 New Hampshire Ave., NW
Washington, D.C. 20036
info@ipsonet.org

ISBN-13: 978-1633910409
ISBN-10: 1633910407

Cover design by Taillefer Long at Illuminated Stories:
www.illuminatedstories.com

Daniel Gutierrez-Sandoval, Executive Director
PSO and Westphalia Press

Devin Proctor, Director of Media and Publications
PSO and Westphalia Press

Updated material and comments on this edition
can be found at the Westphalia Press website:
www.westphaliapress.org

ORIENTAL
RAMBLES

BY

GEORGE W. CALDWELL, M. D.

ILLUSTRATED WITH
NUMEROUS SNAP-SHOT PHOTOGRAPHS

PUBLISHED BY

G. W. CALDWELL, M. D.
POUGHKEEPSIE, N. Y.

G.W. Caldwell. M.D.

INTRODUCTION.

No excuse is offered for this volume and no apology is volunteered. The author did the best he could.

It is not intended as a guide book or a romance, but merely as a true account of the events of travel and the points of interest as the ordinary traveler sees them and his camera portrays them, unhampered by the dry detail of figures, and ungilded by fancy.

THE A. V. HAIGHT COMPANY,
POUGHKEEPSIE, N. Y.

THE A. V. HAIGHT COMPANY,
POUGHKEEPSIE, N. Y.

CONTENTS.

CHAPTER I.

We started westward in October. As we rolled through the beautiful Mohawk Valley glimpses from the car window of the sugar maples flaming with their autumn costumes of red and yellow caused just a little pang of regret for the glorious season we should miss. Perhaps in all the world we should see no more charming sight than that of the woodbine, turned bronze and crimson, festooning the branches of the cedar or the pine tree. When Autumn drapes her gay bunting on the American hillsides all the world should pause and admire, but to us who see this carnival of color every year it is so familiar that its beauties are not properly realized. So we travel, not only to see the wonders and beauties of other countries, but to make us more appreciative of our own. Change keeps the heart young.

One does not fully comprehend what a country is ours until he travels across it. One cannot realize what progress and possibilities are ours unless he remembers that the country through which he passes with its grain fields, its prosperous farm houses, its villages, its factories and its cities with their teeming millions and stupendous commerce were, twenty-five, fifty or seventy-five years ago, only barren plains, prairies or deserts occupied by wild beasts and savages.

On the Oregon Short Line in Idaho there is a railroad eating station built of slabs. In the yard was a bear chained to a stake. A few Indians, wrapped in blankets, asked the passengers for money and got an assortment of things including temperance lectures, chewing tobacco, profanity and cold stares. Whiskey would have pleased them better. The noble red men have fallen on grievous times. Over beyond the sand hills millions of acres of wheat fields have taken the place of their rabbit pastures. Artesian wells, mammoth water reservoirs and canals are turning the deserts into gardens. Peach trees grow where the cactus bristled, and alfalfa flourishes where erstwhile withered the sage brush that was not even fit for goose stuffing.

After the long, hot and dusty ride through the brown Rocky Mountain States, the plunge into the damp, cool and green coast strip of Oregon and Washington was most

refreshing. It is indeed another country.
The stately pines, the rushing waterfalls, the
heights and depths are more majestic than
those of the Adirondacks, or any other eastern region. There is a quality to the western atmosphere that bids one breathe, and
expand, and grow, grow, grow. There is
energy in the air. All nature feels it. The
trees grow larger and taller than elsewhere.
In October, in the wild forest, I saw red and
white clover and grasses of heavier growth
than can be found in the cultivated meadows
of the east. The soil is of incredible depth
and richness. At the green grocer's store
were exposed for sale vegetables and fruits
that would win every prize in an eastern coun-
ty fair, and yet they are ordinary here, and so
cheap that it is foolish to go hungry. Roses
grow like trees on the Pacific coast, and heliotrope hedges are ordinary. The poor little
eastern flowers that are reared so tenderly
in hot houses, and transplanted so carefully
in the spring, and praised so proudly when
promise of a bud appears are, after all, only
insignificant dwarfs when compared to the
sturdy Pacific variety. The west and far
northwest have only begun to grow. The
possibilities are enormous.

CHAPTER II.

At Vancouver the Canadian Pacific Railroad Steamer "Empress of India" awaited the English mail which was rushing across the continent from Montreal twenty-four hours late. The "Empress" looked "kind and sound in wind and limb" as she floated her graceful five hundred feet of length in the waters of Puget Sound. She was white and clean when we went aboard, and no one would suspect she could be restless and "rolly" and "pitchy" and inconsiderate as she proved herself in the north Pacific a few days later. We sailed at five in the afternoon and got a fleeting glimpse of pine-bordered shore, tree-clad mountain ridges and craggy mountain tops before darkness closed upon us.

The captain was going to sail over the top of the earth in order to get around it quicker. In other words, he was to take the shorter northern circle to Yokohama. We had hoped the water would be more level at the top but were disappointed. My personal feelings are of no importance, whatever, but my friend Phil, the Philosopher from Philadelphia, lost his appetite among other things early on the voyage. He denied that he was seasick, but complained that the food was not suitable for his philosophical stomach. He spent much time in enumerating the things he did not know about navigation. The item that troubled him most was, why the ship should be made to reek of disinfectants when any other odor would be preferable even if more deadly.

The passengers who were not seasick conducted themselves in a proud and puissant manner. They went to the dining saloon regularly and brought back the odor of boiled pork and cabbage. They laughed immoderately and looked perniciously cheerful when there was really nothing but sadness and nausea on deck. Our German friend, wrapped in blankets in his steamer chair, expressed our sentiments exactly, when he said as he gazed sadly at the tossing sea, rising and falling with the rolling of the boat:—
"I haf no appetite for such an ocean."

There was a war hero on board. The sword in his strong right hand had mowed down rows of Philippinos. The gatling gun had no terrors for him. Of the bolo he was not afraid, but as he lay wrapped in blankets in a steamer chair on the windward side of the deck the mere mention of cabbage fried with pork would send him flying to the rail where he would tremble and writhe until all was lost save honor.

On shipboard people soon become acquainted. The iceberg social fortifications with which people surround themselves at home melt away at sea. Any one who does not become sociable on a long voyage is not merely frozen but mummified.

When my friend, Phil, the Philosopher from Philadelphia, reeled up on deck one morning he saw a white-faced young woman with her head in the lap of a pale and melancholy-looking young man. They were apparently bride and groom. The Philosopher's tender heart was touched and he said, "Madam, you look ill. Isn't there something I can do for you?"

"No-o," she moaned.

"Can't I get you a cup of bouillon?"

"No-o."

"Well, your husband, he looks ill too; can't I get something for him?"

"No-o, and he isn't my husband, and I don't know who he is."

The best that can be said of the days of this voyage is that they passed with great regularity and solemnity. They were alike in being cold, damp, dreary and sunless. We passed within sight of some of the Aleutian Islands and they did not appear cheerful. There were fire drills occasionally to show what would happen if the ship burned up.

The crew was largely Chinese. All the cooks, dining saloon stewards, and room stewards were Chinese. The passengers were from everywhere. There was a Chinese Mandarin going home under a cloud. In some way he had displeased the Empress and there were strong probabilities that when he should reach Pekin a separation would occur in the neighborhood of his Adam's apple. The Empress has such frolicsome ways with those who please her not. He looked very dignified in his blue silk robes and embroidered skirt, but his mustache had a melancholy droop and his eye a wistful sadness.

On the fifth day out there was a burial at sea. An English lady seventy years of age, traveling around the world with her daughter for pleasure, had suddenly expired on

deck the day before, and just as the cold
morning light was struggling through the
fog the services of burial were held. A British flag was draped over a human form,
wrapped and weighted, lying on a plank by
the rail. The ship's officers stood in line
around it; the engines stopped their throb-
bing; the giant propellers ceased churning
the brine into foam; the ship drifted, and
all was strangely still. A passenger clergy-
man read the burial service of the Church
of England, while the cold and foggy winds
from the north Pacific blew his vestments
about him. All heads were bowed, and at
the words "to the sea we commit her body,"
sailors tilted the plank and the silent form
glided from under the flag and with a splash
disappeared in the sullen waters. There
was a clang of bells, the great propellers
resumed their monotonous grind and the
ship once more moved westward through
the turbulent sea.

When we were in the middle of the Pacific, two thousand miles from America or
Japan, and over a mile to the nearest land
(straight down) a strange thing happened.
We mislaid a day—lost it. At the one hundred and eightieth degree of longitude we

missed it. It suddenly disappeared. At thirteen minutes after two o'clock Sunday it instantly became Monday at the same hour. The only way to recover it was to go back and pick it up.

The Philosopher had a new scheme for perpetual youth. All he needed was an airship that would sail around the world in twenty-four hours. Then, by sailing westward, and keeping under the sun, night would never come, and so no days could be charged up against his age.

"But," I objected. "You will trip up on this line and lose a day. This one hundred eightieth meridan was evidently put here to foil just such a scheme."

"It wouldn't foil me," he declared. "I wouldn't cross it at all; I'd go around it."

At last we sighted land and after steaming along the coast for several hours came to rest in the crowded roadstead of Yokohama. Among the ships of many nations that were in the harbor were some of the Japanese war vessels that surprised the world by their victories over the Russians. Steam tenders landed us at the dock and after a few formalities with the polite customs officials we stepped into jinrikishas, and the little brown men with bare muscular legs drew us at a rapid trot along the street skirting the water front to the Grand Hotel, and the first stage of our trip was over.

CHAPTER III.

From my window at the Grand Hotel I looked out upon a strange sight. It was indeed Japan. At the hotel entrance a group of rikisha men awaited their fares as cabmen do in America, but they were not like the crowding banditti that shout "Keb? Keb?" in the face of a foreigner at the stations or docks in New York, for when one emerges from the hotel these rikisha men will merely smile, and bow, and point to their respective rikishas without offering any physical violence.

If you should step into one of the vehicles, the lucky owner will bow again, and placing himself between the shafts will run as swiftly as Mercury on the wings of the wind and you arrive at your destination with a flourish, and as quickly as with a horse. For the ride, including the politeness, only five cents is asked, and ten expected. In this cold season their short muscular legs were encased in skin tight blue cotton trousers and they wore jackets of the same material, but in the hot

19

season they divest themselves of much more than the law would allow in America.

There were children in the street; myriads of them. They seemed to run in pairs, for nearly every urchin had a baby strapped to its little back and the two were inclosed in a single padded kimona. The effect was a little startling at first, for it appeared that for every pair of legs there were two heads. It was sometimes puzzling to tell which head belonged to the legs. The children looked like the Japanese dolls that are sold in America. They had the chubby round faces, shaven scalps, (excepting the top knot,) almond shaped, bright eyes, and flat small noses of the dolls. And how they could run,—but not faster than their noses.

Phil, the Philosopher, said that hereafter his donations to the missionary fund would be limited to handkerchiefs.

There was a canal at the side of the hotel and on it passed the curious sanpans or boats propelled with an oar or sweep at the stern. Larger ones were rigged with square sails upon which were painted the criss-cross puzzles that serve as characters of the language.

Over beyond on the brow of the hill stood a temple, grey with age. The carved wooden

There Were Children in the Street.

dragons on the gables and rafters glared across the expanse of tiled roofs. Nearby was a solitary pine tree. Its long branches stretched across the temple entrance as if in benediction upon the natives as they passed in and out. It was just at sunset. The sky was a riot of colors. From the temple came the deep tones of a gong that lingered in the air with mellow reverberations.

CHAPTER IV.

YOKOHAMA—JAPAN AWAKENED.

The modernization of Japan began only fifty years ago when Parry anchored his imposing fleet in Mississippi Bay near Yokohama, and by the most clever diplomacy negotiated a treaty by which certain ports were to be opened to the commerce of the world. This terminated the policy of non-communication with the outer world to which Japan had adhered for two hundred years or more.

During these fifty odd years Japan has advanced from the feudal form of government, similar to that of the middle ages in Europe, to a government with one of the most liberal constitutions of the world. From the different countries she has chosen the best models for adoption into her commmercial and political life. She has won two great wars on land and sea. She has earned and compelled the consideration and respect of all nations.

When the Japanese were known only as the greatest artists in the world we considered them heathen, but now that they have proven that they can also fight, and have killed and maimed hundreds of thousands of

Russians, and taken by force countries that did not belong to them, we acknowledge them civilized, and award them a place in the family group of nations.

Those who would see Japan with the picturesque and romantic atmosphere of the ancient times should go at once. The electric lights will soon make the paper lanterns seem dim, and the trolley cars and the automobiles will given even the rikisha men a hard race. The kimonas are passing. The ugly derby hat and other European abominations are more and more in evidence. The Japanese long to learn and advance in European civilization. Clothes help the cause along although the people lose in appearance and comfort by the change.

One may well spend several days wandering about the streets of Yokohama. It is all so new and so delightful.

The Benton Dori, and Honcho Dori are streets in the native quarter devoted to the curio trade, and there one may wander for hours studying the strange and beautiful goods of the olden time. Some may not be as old as they look, for real antiques are getting scarce. However who would object to a really beautiful antique merely because it is new! Certainly not Phil, the Philosopher. He has a passion for antiques. He has acquired a nice wooden idol with an extended palm, which is, strange to say, wrong side up. That is sufficient evidence that it is not genuine.

Poor Phil, in Egypt he purchased a mummified sacred hawk, guaranteed to be several thousand years antique, but alas, it proved too new and he had to throw it overboard at sea.

The curio shops are open in front to the streets and you are welcome to enter, and wander about, and inspect to your heart's content. The shop-keeper bows, and smiles, and sucks the air through his teeth in the most polite "Jappy" fashion, and asks ten times as much as he expects to get.

The labor expended on some trifle of carving or embroidery is so great, and the price so small that one is tempted to buy and buy until extra baggage accumulates and bids him stop. Ivories, wonderfully carved—porcelains, exquisitely painted—bronzes, cloisonne, lacquer, ancient arms, and embroideries that are marvels of beauty, fascinate and nothing but the joy of possession will satisfy the traveler.

Street Scene.

"Crick Sole. Small Profit."

CHAPTER V.

A few hours railroad ride across the rice fields brings one to Tokio, the capital. Japan being a mountainous country with a large population every spot of tillable land is cultivated to the highest degree. The soil is broken, not by plows or spades, but by a long heavy hoe. The lands that can be flooded are planted by hand to rice, and the elevated spots and terraces to vegetables. The rice when ripe is reaped, bundled and hung on bamboo poles or trees planted for the purpose, to dry. When cured the rice is threshed by women who draw the straw, a few spears at a time, through iron combs and then winnow the grain in the wind or with hand bellows. The straw is used for thatch, rope making, sandals, paper, etc. Nothing is wasted. Vegetables are thickly planted. Every inch of soil is utilized. A monster radish, called the daikon, is one of the staple foods.

The cottages of the farmers reflect the artistic and aesthetic nature of the people.

Humble though the home may be—its two or three small rooms constructed of straw, bamboo and paper—there will be a minature flower garden—only four or five feet square perhaps, but complete with walks, lakes, arched bridges and with trees and flowers dwarfed to correspond to the scale.

The Japanese are liberal advertisers and the landscape is enlivened with larger signs than seen in America extolling the virtues of beer, biscuits and tobacco. Japanese characters made of painted stones on a distant hillside remind the traveler what to take for "that tired feeling."

Railroad station scenes are always interesting. Japanese women run when going to or from a train. Short steps are required because their knees are bound by tight kimonas. The scuffling of sandals that drag at the heel, and the clatter of wooden clogs become familiar sounds. Japanese crowds are always good natured. In fact good nature and courtesy are the characteristics most in evidence. They lead the simple life, live close to nature, and have a keen sense of the humorous as well as the artistic. I have seen grown men rest in their labor of carrying brick, take a top from a pocket and spin it with the merriment of children for a few minutes, then resume their work. It is strange that such gentle people should be such invincible warriors. They have never known defeat, and in the hour of their greatest victories they have surprised the world by the modesty of their demands, their kindness to prisoners and their generosity to their fallen foe.

Intellectually the Japanese are at least equal to any race. They are better students. Education is universal. Their schools are on model lines. Children may be seen in the school yards drilling in military tactics. Their civilization is not new. The Japanese enjoyed books, arts and silks while Europeans were still savages dressed in skin.

To the Japanese patriotism is not only the greatest virtue, but the fundamental principle of their Shinto religion. The old Samauri class, or soldier knights, considered that their lives belonged to their feudal lords. Feudalism has been abolished and the clans disbanded, but the spirit of Samauri still lives in the hearts of the people. Any citizen would consider it an honor to die for his country. During the war there was no lack of volunteers. The most dangerous duty was sought as a favor. Women sent all the males of the family that would be taken. Women did the men's work and even attempted to reach the fighting line. It is said that women after giving their men and their money even sold themselves to the Yoshawara to get more money to give to the cause.

The Yoshawara is a city within the city. It has high inclosing walls with a single gate. Within this wall are many streets of·three or four story houses. There are said to be twenty thousand women in the Yoshawara. They are sold for a certain period for purposes of public immorality and when that period has expired they return to their homes, marry and do not suffer the social ostracism that would follow such a life in America or Europe. If necessary for the support of parents it is considered a filial duty, and a pious act, for a daughter to sell herself to the Yoshawara, that her parents may not want. They are more often sold by parents or guardians. The Yoshawara women are known by their obie, or broad sash, being tied in front instead of the back as respectable women wear it. They are licensed and supervised by the government.

The Japanese take the position that since the social evil must and does exist in all countries either openly or secretly, it is better, sociologically, that it be sequestered, and under medical and police control.

Most travelers, men and women, do not think the visit to Tokio complete unless they walk or ride through the streets of the Yoshawara in the evening. The streets are brilliantly lighted and thronged by an orderly crowd. The street floor of the houses are open to the sidewalk except for a grating. Behind this grating with a setting like a stage of a comic opera are groups of Musmees in resplendent kimonas with faces painted white with rice powder, lips crimsoned, and hair wonderfully arranged in puffs and wings stiff with paste and glittering with tinsel hair pins. A half dozen girls may be arrayed in lilac kimonas, a half dozen in rose and another bevy in dove color. They amuse themselves by smoking the universal long-stem small pipes that hold tobacco enough for only two or three puffs, when the ashes are knocked out on the side of the charcoal brasier that serves also as a hand warmer. Others may be playing on the seimsen—a form of guitar. They are picturesque, in no way vulgar or rude, and are much amused at the efforts of foreigners to say the few words of Japanese they think they know.

Many Europeans sojourning in Japan contract Japanese marriages, taking advantage of the extremely easy divorce system which requires no legal formalities. In spite of the fact, that marriage may be dissolved at the good pleasure of the husband, such separations are extremely rare among the Japanese themselves. There a man is truly "master in his own house." No matter how wrong her husband may be a wife must always consider him right, and his will as law. There can, therefore, be no quarrelling or bickering in a Japanese family. In spite of this strange condition the women do not seem to have discovered how unhappy they are, but appear the merriest and happiest women in the world. In spite of all these precautions taken for their protection, Japanese men are led around by the cord on the heart, or pushed along with a club on the back, by women just as they are in other countries.

The Japanese are passionately fond of flowers. Business men and all classes of so-

A Tragedy in Chrysanthemums.

In Theatre Street.

ciety suspend duties to make a holiday in honor of the cherry blossoms. When the wistaria blooms, or the plums blossom, or the chrysanthemum blooms, flower festivals are held. All the phases of nature are watched with interest. Their admiration for nature amounts almost to worship. Family crests are usually conventional designs of flowers, for instance the Shoguns crest is three leaves of the hydrangea inclosed in a circle. The Emperor's is a sixteen petaled chrysanthemum.

Late in October there was a chrysanthemum show in Ueno Park. It was more like an exposition. Innumerable banners fluttered from forests of bamboo poles and decorated the entrances to the booths that crowded each side of the street. A ticket-seller at each booth loudly proclaimed the superior merits of his show and sold for a penny a wooden ticket large enough to be worth that for firewood. He also presented a program and among the Japanese advertisements I noticed a cut of a large bottle with the legend in English "Try Scott's Emulsion."

The chrysanthemums themselves were not as large as those grown in hot houses in

America, but they were displayed in wonderful quantities and strange designs. They were used principally to cover set pieces in tableau. Entire scenes from the theatre, with all the characters made of blooms, were set on circular stages that revolved at short intervals, battle scenes, and mythological legends being largely represented. There was a striking tableau of a maiden with a wax face and chrysanthemum kimona, standing under a blooming cherry tree, bidding good-bye to a floral soldier, with a floral Fuji in the background. It seemed to be a glorified Eden Musee in flowers. There was a naval battle scene with chrysanthemum battleships in deadly combat, in which, of course, the Russian chrysanthemum ships were sinking in a chrysanthemum sea.

CHAPTER VI.

THE EMPEROR'S BIRTHDAY—JAPAN TRI-UMPHANT.

The Emperor's birthday, November third, is a holiday in Japan. The Emperor reviews the army in the morning and there is a state ball in the evening.

At seven thirty o'clock we left the Imperial hotel in rikishas, proceeding at the usual brisk run to the field. The streets were swarming with people. Flags and bunting were floating to the breeze from every building. Leaving the rikishas at the entrance we entered the field between columns of military guards, and proceeded to the part reserved for foreigners. This was near a corner of a square of perhaps a half mile to each side.

To the right was the Imperial tent, and spaces reserved for foreign diplomats. On the opposite side was drawn up the artillery and cavalry, while on the right and left sides were massed many regiments of infantry. This army of upward fifty thousand veterans stood as rigid as statues. They were awaiting the Emperor. Beyond the soldiers were thousands of citizens, men, women, and children, and in the distance Fugiyama reared its snowy cone twelve thousand feet into the blue sky.

Through the gates came a multitude of notables—army and navy officers in brilliant uniforms, foreign diplomats and military attachees. The uniforms of all nations seemed to be represented. The Chinese officers and diplomats in magnificent brocades, satins and furs, and with peacock feathers in their caps were gorgeous as a millinery store.

An hour passed. The soldiers stood like statues; not a military knee had moved; with all these thousands assembled there was not a sound; not a voice; not a murmur; not a drum had rolled; not even an eye had rolled.

At last there was a bugle note. An officer extraordinarily braided with gold rode through the gate followed by a company of cavalry with lances. Then followed the Imperial outriders, and the Imperial coach in which sat "The Dragon's Eye," the one hundred and twenty-first reigning descendent of the Sun Goddess—The Mikado of Japan. Instantly all heads were uncovered. The

Emperor, stern of visage, generous of girth, his strong intellectual face scantily bewhiskered, looked every inch a king. He bowed kindly to the right and left as he passed rapidly to the Imperial tent. There he mounted a waiting horse and followed by a body of officers began the march at a walk around the square. The military band the while playing the national air, a solemn chant suggestive of the dead march from Saul.

The circuit being completed he took a position in front of his tent while the troops marched in review before him to the lively music with which they had gone to battle in Manchuria.

The maneuvering of this immense body of men, horses and artillery with clock work precision and great rapidity was in itself a demonstration of its effectiveness and an explanation for is successes. There were no delays, no gaps, no hitches. They marched in close formation, double quick. The review was all over in a few minutes. A powerful army had passed. No wonder such an army could march around the Russians and strike where least expected.

We left the field before the crowd dispersed to avoid the rush. In spite of that we were caught between two streams of humanity, but the crowd was good natured and orderly. The Japanese are probably the cleanest people in the world, both in their bodies and clothing. Consequently close crowding is not as abhorent as in some other countries. Profane and vulgar words are not known, at least so the guide said. I hope this is true, but he also said there is no lying, which sounded Irish to the Philosopher.

The policemen carried ponderous swords at their belts, but were punctiliously polite to the people. At one point the police were to hold back the crowd from passing through a certain street, but when the crowd broke through, the policemen bowed and allowed them to pass without breaking any heads, maiming any children, arresting any women, or using words that would cause the angels to put cotton in their ears.

CHAPTER VII.

If there is an enchanted forest it is Nikko. If castles could be conjured from the caves of magic, nothing more elaborate could be imagined than its temples. Nikko means "sun brightness" and there is a Japanese saying "Use not the word beautiful, until you have seen Nikko." Every turn in the avenues of giant evergreens brings new and wonderful scenes,—rushing torrents, tinkling cascades, mossy stone idols on ferny banks, temples, pavilions, pagodas or entrancing views of mountains and valleys.

In the dark and mysterious shade of ancient pines are temples so elaborately carved, gilded and lacquered that they seem more like the jewel boxes of the Gods than the handiwork of man, and about them is that indescribable solemnity which casts a spell like that of the interior of a great cathedral. But cathedrals in cities are so palpably artificial, while Nikko seems so near to nature that it might have grown as the flowers grow, and its temples have been crystallized from the essence of beauty after a million years of refinement in the studio of nature.

When one views St. Peter's in Rome, or St. Paul's in London, or the Temple of Karnak in Upper Egypt, words come freely enough—grand, imposing, enormous. But when one stands before that marble miracle of the Taj in India, or a tiny temple at Nikko, words fail. To them shall be paid the supreme compliment of silent awe. .To them shall be admitted the defeat of words; but a rapture fills the soul, and the mind is humbled befitting an approach to the deity. Such creations are in themselves a worship as they were truly intended. Yet each of these we call heathen because they approach the deity by another road than the one we, ourselves, have constructed. Can the Great Spirit of Love—the Creator of Nature's laws—be so particular by what name he is addressed, or the form used in addressing him, provided all forms are equally sincere and worshipful?

Before an image of Buddha a native was praying. He held in his hand a silken tassel and as he repeated a prayer he turned down a thread. There were hundreds of threads. His face denoted intense devotional concentration and a high degree of spirituality. He was in no way disturbed by the presence of our party, indeed he seemed to be unaware of our presence. A good lady turned away with a look of abhorrence and remarked:

"Poor heathen, how ignorant. Can't he see them idols is dumb?"

I wonder how the recording angel cast up the account. Perhaps the good-hearted soul is even now discoursing to some missionary circle how she saw the heathen bowing down to idols of wood and stone, but her explanation may not include the fact that these heathen ladies and gentlemen no more worship the idol than Christians worship idols when they pray before the cross, or crucifix, or the altar. In both cases it is merely a symbol to assist in concentrating the mind on the deity. The image is not a God, or the image of a God, but merely the image or statue of a man, Gautama Buddha, who founded Buddhism in India six hundred years before Christ, and whose followers number nearly one-third of the world's population.

There is a striking resemblance between Buddhist and Catholic religious services. Each has the incense, bells, candles, images and processions, and each has a priesthood wearing distinctive robes and leading lives of celibacy and charity. They have monasteries and schools and attain a state of eternal rest and blessedness, not by the vicarious sacrifice of a Redeemer, or the intervention of saints, but by enlightenment, self denial and pure living.

It is curious what different ideas devotees of different religions have of heaven. To the Buddhist it is Nirvana, the calm of perfect rest; to the ancient Norsemen it was a land of perpetual summer; to the Mohammedan it is a palace of sensual delights; while to the Hebrew, it is a city with golden streets, pearly gates, jasper seas, and the pomps and ceremonies of a King of Jerusalem. In these luxurious days of the twentieth century any ordinary millionaire can come very near buying any of these delightful conditions except the Buddhist's.

The great Tycoon Iyeyasu is buried at Nikko. A temple of lacquer and gold does him honor. Innumerable bronze lanterns, offerings of his loving admirers, stand in rows and avenues. A white pony with blue eyes is kept saddled and bridled in a building near by ready for the hero in case he should decide to return to earth.

A Temple Gate at Nikko.

This stable for the sacred horse is also a marvel of carving and lacquer. On it are the famous monkeys of Nikko, which are more celebrated than the bronze lanterns, or the elephant whose hind legs bend the wrong way because the artist was left handed.

This carving represents three monkeys in a tree. One holds his hands over his ears and an inscription reads "Hear no evil," another covers his eyes with his hands and the inscription reads "See no evil," while the third covers his mouth with his hands and the inscription reads "Speak no evil." They illustrate the Japanese saying, "Hear not too much, see not too much, speak not too much."

To enter a temple one must remove the shoes. One must also remove the shoes to enter the house of the humblest native. Shoes and sandals are for the dirt, and dirt is not for the house. To a Japanese his floor is also his chair and his table. But there are special reasons for removing shoes in these temples. The floors are covered with priceless lacquers polished like the finest piano. Pillars are covered with inches of lacquer, at fabulous expense, and then carved, showing the colors of the successive layers of lacquer.

The wonders of the temple, its art objects and its relics were shown us. We were a band of foreigners, ignorant in things Japanese, not of their religion, and some of us not over respectful, but the priest was polite, considerate and, even indulgent. The one who can venerate the sacred objects of another is a great man. How much these priests have to bear from some disrespectful foreigners may be judged by the following extracts from the book of a well known English author:

"You buy your ticket, a little piece of coarse paper, with its contents for a wonder in Japanese only, and sealed and counter-sealed with funny little red ink seals to prevent the attendants embezzling the money, and you enter with a guide who only talks Japanese and smiles like a seraph, while the Philistine pokes fun at him in English. This I noticed and felt, like the Pharisee, on the verge of uttering thanks that I was not like these Publicans. It really was solemn to me."

You will be glad he was solemn when you learn how he got in, which he relates on the preceding page of his book in the following shocking confession, which will be better un-

derstood if I explain that to enter the sacred
groves and temple grounds one must pass a
small river or torrent. For this purpose, on
the main road, a bridge is provided. It is
broad, and solid, and safe and good enough
for even an author. Near this is the sacred
bridge used only by the Mikado in ceremonials. This sacred bridge is out of the way,
inconvenient to reach, gated and locked at
both ends, and respected by all natives.
Now read the advice of this celebrated English author:

"At the bridge, dismount and send your
rikisha and baggage to the hotel to wait
for you, then *break the law*.* Traffic does
not cross Mihashi, the exquisite red lacquer
sacred bridge springing from shore to shore
with a single span like the arc of a rainbow,
supported at each end by a gigantic double torii
of grey granite. But over this airy structure
the bodies of Iyeyasu and his descendants,
living and dead, had been borne for more
than two centuries before their dynasty
fell. Therefore, *break the law,** and climbing over the feeble gates, enter the holy
ground of Nikko by the sacred bridge."

*Italics mine.—*G. W. C.*

Fortunately for the traveling public such law breakers are rare. When General Grant visited Japan he was accompanied to Nikko by a delegation from the Imperial household. As a mark of great honor he was presented with an Edict of the Mikado throwing open the sacred bridge to him. After reading the translation he puffed violently at his cigar and declared, "I will be the last person to break a law of Japan," and crossed the public bridge.

CHAPTER VIII.

From Yokohama there are many side trips for a day about which chapters might well be written.

Kamakura was an ancient capital and a stronghold, but now the plains where a million people lived are only rice fields and vegetable gardens. Civil wars, earthquakes and tidal waves have done their work, and only the Gods remain. These are perhaps the most eminent Gods in all Japan. Tidal waves have destroyed the temples that covered the Great Buddha, but its enormous weight has defied time and waves for five hundred years. It is a bronze sitting figure fifty feet high. Visitors may sit upon his thumb for photographs.

Nearby are parts of the ancient temple of Hachiman, the war hero, with the arms and trophies of many great soldiers guarded by priests.

On a hillock protected by a shed-like temporary structure stands Kwannon, the Goddess of Mercy, in wood carving overlaid with gold. She is thirty feet high and hundreds of years old. Fires and floods have destroyed the temple that covered her, but they have been merciful to the "Lady of Mercy."

There is Miyanoshita, that delightful nook in the mountains, where we lingered a week reveling in the scenery and parboiling in the natural hot springs. The waters from the hot springs are piped directly into the hotel to supply the cement tanks in the bathing compartments.

This hotel is "Jappier" than other semi-foreign hotels at which we had stopped. Nearly all the service is performed by pretty little girls who cluster about like butterflies and seem everywhere present. Their round, laughing faces frequently appeared at the most unexpected times,—even when the rites of the bath were being performed, or during the ceremony of dressing, so sacred to an American. They meant no harm. It is the custom of the country.

Across the street was a public bath for the common people. It was half open to the the street. There males and females of all ages plunged about in the tanks in the costume fashionable in the Garden of Eden before the fall. They paid no more attention to each other than would children.

My rikisha man was very much amused at my inquiry if there was no impropriety about it. The idea seemed never to have occurred to him. "Would foreigners see anything wrong in it?" he asked. It was plain he thought foreigners must be a very evil-minded lot.

The air was chill. Overcoats were necessary for our comfort, and yet in the early morning Japanese men could be seen darting out of the bath-house, their nude bodies red as boiled lobsters, and carrying their kimonas on their arms, they would run down the streets to their homes as fast as their legs could carry them.

At the side of the hotel was a deep ravine. Everywhere the hillsides are so steep that were it not for the dense tangle of scrub bamboo their sides would wash into the valleys. Springs gushed from the hillsides and babbling waters could be heard day and night. In the ravine was a brawling brook. Its course could be traced from far up the mountain side. The gleaming foam of the torrent, like a silver thread, was woven in and out among the rich colors, gold and bronze and crimson, of the autumnal brocade. Down across the ravine the steep hill-side looked like a mammoth picture in a frame of pines hung against the sky, so lavishly were the colors poured upon the verdure.

A favorite walk was up the ravine to the tea house of the gold fish. There one can drink the weak tea of the country and learn Japanese from the dainty musmees who serve it; and feed little cakes to the gold fish in the fountain. This is said to have been a favorite resort of Sir Edwin Arnold. A more poetical spot can scarcely be imagined.

In chairs slung on poles and carried by coolies, picnic excursions were made to charming waterfalls, and to Lake Hakone from which a good view was obtained of snow-capped Fiji. Crossing the lake in sampans, as the small boats are called, we were met by another set of carriers who carried us back to Miyanoshita via "Hell."

There are two hells, called big and little. Little hell is a small affair of sulphur springs and steam, but the "Big Hell" is a terror. Here a volcano must come very near the surface. Over acres there is no vegetation.

By Mountain Waterfalls.

All is dreary and desolate; birds will not approach it. The ground is a hot crust and resounds under the feet with a hollow sound and a disquieting vibration. Every few feet there is a vent through which comes hissing, and hot from the caldron below sulphurous vapors, which, cooling in the air, turn white and deposit cones of sulphur like miniature volcanoes. This sulphur is gathered up, and sold, and thus even "Hell" pays tribute to this thrifty people.

When we had passed this inferno and resumed our chairs we were carried by these surefooted mountaineers rapidly along paths on the brink of cliffs, and across mountain torrents on fallen trees. It looked dangerous, but having passed safely through the realms of Beelzebub, what else was there that could terrify us.

It was with regret that we said "sayonara" to the smiling and bowing "musmees" who lined up at the hotel door to bid us goodbye. The air was clear, the morning crisp, and our rikisha men fairly galloped with us down the mountain road to the station with the unpronounceable name, where we took the train for Kioto.

The journey was broken by a day at Shid-

zuoka and another at Nagoya, where we saw
ancient castles and temples. When we
reached the comfortable hotel in Kioto we
realized with regret that half of our journey
in Japan was over.

CHAPTER IX.

Kioto was the capital of Japan for a thousand years, and abounds in temples and aristocracy. We had been advised to defer purchases of silks and embroideries until we reached Kioto. Our guide said we could get there "also curios more antique."

During the morning we roamed about old temples and gardens and castles. In the afternoon we rummaged among the curio shops and silk stores. Such beautiful things were temptations too strong to resist, and no one should resist, for trifles in Japan become art treasures in America.

After Nikko there is not much to be said of temples. There are many larger but none so beautiful. One large and beautiful temple has recently been completed at a cost of over eight million dollars,—an immense sum in this country where the people are poor. It was built entirely from gifts from the people. The rich gave money or material; the poor gave their labor. Women cut off their hair and sent it to be woven into

51

ropes for hoisting materials. Coils of this rope are preserved as relics. This seems to contradict the statement frequently made that the old religions are being displaced by Christianity.

A Buddhist theological seminary connected with the temple of Nishi Hongwanji is actually preparing students to be sent into Christian countries as missionaries. In fact foreign missions are already established. A priest remarked, "If you send men to convert us, why should we not pay you the same attention, as we know our religion is more ancient and logical than yours."

I wonder if Americans would be as tolerant of a "Joss House" set up in their neighborhood and making an energetic campaign for converts as these Japanese, or even the Chinese, are of Christian missions.

The temples of Shinto, the ancient religion of Japan, are exceedingly simple. Before each stands a tori, or arch, which is merely two upright posts connected by two beams at the top—the upper beam curved with the concavity upward. Tassels of rice straw decorate it. The temple itself is merely a pavilion. There is a contribution box, a bell and a mirror. The worshiper enters the temple,

The Buddha in the Temple Yard.

tosses a contribution into the box, strikes the gong to ring up the Gods, and gazes into the mirror. If he sees no sin in himself then he goes his way in peace, but if in this self-examination he finds error, he must correct it. The creed is exceedingly simple, the spirit of which is, honor the Emperor, and your parents and go not contrary to your own conscience.

The earlier wars of Japan on the mainland of Asia were not conducted on the humane principles of the last. A mound was pointed out to us in which were buried thousands of ears taken from slain Coreans, three hundred and fifty years ago. Since that time Corea has lent her ears when Japan gave advice. Lending is better than losing.

It was Russia's attempt to gather in Corea that sent Japan grappling at the throat of the giant bear—a bear which kills its own cubs.

There is an interesting trip to Lake Biwa to see the giant pine tree with branches two hundred and eighty feet long which need to be supported to prevent their breaking down. Its trunk is about forty feet around, but it is only a hundred feet high. It seems to have run to width like an alderman.

A ride down the rapids of Katsuragawa is an exciting experience. It is a thirteen mile "shoot the shutes" with curves and rocks and other dangers in the mountain passes. The guide said dragons had been seen in the dark places. (A dragon is a sort of a lobster. It appears in dreams after welsh rarebit suppers.)

Kioto is a good place to go to theatres, music halls, wrestling matches, dinners and other dissipations. We saw a tragedy and enjoyed it. Imagine a tragedian strutting about the stage with a candle on the end of a stick held in front of his face that the audience may see his terrible grimaces. The super who holds the candle is invisible. You know he is invisible because he wears a sign that says so.

The Japanese have no idea of stage lighting. They have no footlights, side, top or spot lights, but hang candles, lanterns and electric arc lights in a jumble in front of the stage, an arrangement which both lights the stage and blinds the audience. However, for bona fide melodrama, with villains in all their fifty-seven varieties, helpless females, and dashing heroes, the Japanese brand is hard to beat.

At the music hall may be seen some very picturesque dancing. Some of the classical descriptive dances are pleasing and artistic, but the music,—the squeaky, screechy music,—how can it be described? Phil, the Philosopher, says he now comprehends why the Buddhist longs for Nirvana, the calm of perfect rest.

In this music hall there was a ladies' orchestra. Their seimsens twanged like broken banjos, their tom-toms thumped, and the shrieks of their bamboo flutes tore dreadful holes in the atmosphere, while a bevy of pretty musmees sang, or rather squeaked like mice.

The dancing is of the kind peculiar to the far eastern countries. It consists of a series of graceful poses, turning of the hands and arms, coquetting with a fan, an occasional rotation of the body, and lifting of a knee, with the foot turned in and the great toe erect as though the dancer had stepped on a tack. The last position indicates mirth and jollity.

CHAPTER X.

Osaka is a sort of Asiatic Venice, grid-ironed as it is with canals, but instead of the tumble down palaces of a worn out nobility there are the factories and storehouses of commercial Japan.

The Japanese have two classes of art goods; one for the Japanese, and on that they spend an incredible amount of patient and wonderfully skillful labor. For this the Japanese themselves pay good prices. The other class of goods is for "export only." No Japanese would tolerate it. This is practically the only class of Japanese goods we see in the stores in America. These goods are coarse and garish with gilt and colors.

In the loft we found a factory, or studio, for modern Satsuma ware. Here artists, working with magnifying glasses, were painting miniature scenes and figures with wonderful detail; for instance one artist was painting an entire religious procession with hundreds of figures and portraits on a tiny vase, no larger than a tea cup. This would require weeks of time, and the price would make it unsalable in Europe or America, except perhaps to an art collector.

There is an ancient fortress in Osaka impregnable in the olden times of bows, arrows and swords, but taken easily enough now-a-days even by a tourist with a camera. It has immense walls, some stones of which are forty feet long by twelve feet high and ten feet thick. Others at the corners of the gates are twenty feet high, veritable cliffs in themselves. Yet they were brought from distant island quarries before the time of machinery.

The street signs in Japanese-English were a constant source of amusement. The Japanese is a good imitator, but never gets it exact. That is very well with merchandise, but with the English language it is ludicrous. The Jap who has learned a little English assumes that he knows the language and proceeds to mutilate it without mercy. Here is a shop sign in Osaka:

O. KOMAI,
Monoplist of Milk.

Another was more true and appropriate than the proprietor probably surmised:

> HERE ONE DOES EUROPEANS,
> Curios, things encien.

This style of left handed English is not limited to the small shops. I have a recepted bill from one of the largest silk and curio stores in Kioto as follows:

> " 2 hangings I got from artist Kobun and he execute by orders from Prince Nabeshima."

The above referred to two painted silk curtains and not to a legal execution as might be inferred.

My camera films and prints came back from a leading photographer, where they had been sent to be developed and printed. They were enclosed in an envelope, beautifully embossed in Japanese characters, and the English script "potograph."

At a rikisha stand the tariff of charges is explained on a bulletin in the following lucid English:

> "The rikisha charge is by two man for to
> go up one yen also likewise for to come down.
> By night and if storm more is double."

At Kobe we went to see the peculiar Japanese roosters which grow tail feathers fifteen feet long.   These birds conducted themselves with great dignity, trailing their tails
and bestowing as much care in their manage-
ment as European ladies do with their trains.
Perhaps this is the original phoenix bird,
which, with the dragon, figures so largely in
Japanese and Chinese art.

CHAPTER XI.

At Kobe we took steamer and sailed through the Inland Sea to Nagasaki. This is a most delightful voyage suggestive at times of the Thousand Islands in the St. Lawrence, Lake George or Lake Champlain, and again broadening out until one might fancy he was sailing the waters of Puget Sound until an approach to the land in a narrow passage brought to view the torii and temples that are unmistakably Japanese. But the shipping does not let one forget it is Japan. The high-sterned junks with their square sails bring to mind the childhood stories of the "blood-thirsty pirates that scour the southern seas."

As we neared Nagasaki we passed picturesque islands and rugged headlands. One sheer cliff projecting into the sea is called Pappenburg Rock. Over it were hurled thousands of native Christians, converts of the Portuguese and Spanish Jesuits, four hundred years ago. At that time Japan had more than a million Catholics and Catholicism was growing rapidly, but they meddled in politics and the Shoguns suspected that it was the intent of the foreigners to reduce Japan to a dependency of the King of Spain, as had been done with the Philippines and other countries. Then they were completely wiped out, and the country closed to foreign relations. It remained so until the year eighteen hundred and fifty-four, when Perry negotiated the famous epoch-making treaty of amity and commerce with the United States.

The harbor of Nagasaki is the most picturesque in all Japan, its encircling hill being terraced and set with temples.

As soon as our ship had anchored, we were surrounded by a flotilla of coal barges on which were hundreds of chattering women in blue cotton kimonas. The barges were quickly lashed to the side, ladders placed, and the little women passed baskets of coal so rapidly from hand to hand that it fell in a steady cataract into the bunkers.

We hastened on shore where we took riki-shas to see as many of the sights as the few hours stop-over of the steamer would allow.

At first we went to the temple of the

Sacred Horse. Sacred horses are common enough but bronze ones are rare, so we climbed the hundreds of stone steps under many torii of stone and bronze to the Shinto Temple at the top of the hill.

The famed bronze horse is not much of a success. Japanese horses are the worst in the world, but this is an unflattering likeness. It seems to have a little hippopotamus blood in it. In an adjoining court there is a real live sacred horse. It is an albino, with weak, watery eyes, mangy coat and a generally disreputable and unsanctified appearance.

Nearby is a tree planted by General Grant and the house built for his entertainment. Japan spared no expense in the honor of the Great American. His remark at the sacred bridge at Nikko was only one of the ways by which he endeared himself to the Japanese people.

After luncheon we visited the "Tea House of the Garden of Flowers," made famous by Pierre Loti in his book "Madame Chrysanthemum." From this tea house there was a charming panorama of forest-clad hills almost surrounding the harbor, where floated the ships of many nations. The city was spread out like a map below. Beyond the

The Bronze Horse.

harbor entrance were islands studding the bay, and stretching away to the western horizon were the blue waters of the China Sea.

As we sailed out of the harbor, bound for Shanghai, the sunset was draping the hills with golden brown in the sunlit ridges, and misty purple in the shadowy ravines.

Into the west we sailed, into a sea of gold, and silver, and turquois. The sweet reverberations of the bell of a distant hillside temple came to us over the waters, lingering in the air, and causing a pang of sadness, a sigh of regret that we were at last parting, perhaps forever, with dear old Japan.

There are many things, dear old Japan, of which we may have complained unjustly or treated too lightly, but your people are a kind, courteous and pleasant people. Your most cruel sports are top-spinning and kite-flying. Your vocabularly is complete without profanity. You torture trees into dwarf and grotesque shapes, but you make no distortion of the human body. You see no evil in nature's laws. Your list of mortal sins is not so long that you are forever sad with the contemplation of them. You go through life laughing and bowing. You see beauty in the flight of the stork, a sermon in the pine tree and a poem in every blossom.

Sayonara rikishas; Sayonara, tea houses, with the saffron colored tea; Sayonara, geishas, and musmees. May we meet again when the wistaria's radiant clusters beckon from the trellis, and the cherry blossoms come.

CHAPTER XII.

SHANGHAI, OLD AND NEW.

On the morning of the second day we awoke to find the ship anchored in the muddy waters of the Yang-tse River at Woo Sung. Low lying mud banks were visible far away on each side.

Native boats clustered around from one of which an ancient Chinaman in a wadded jacket climbed over the side. He sat down on the deck unceremoniously, and proceeded to take from his mouth and ears a surprising quantity of paraphernalia with which he performed many mystifying tricks of slight of hand. The things he could do with a whip and top seemed to upset all laws of gravitation. After this he set himself on fire inside. Flames and smoke poured from his mouth. He belched fire like a volcano. Then he drew forth great quantities of curled papers, and finally a huge bunch of firecrackers just in time to have them explode on the outside. What would have happened if they had exploded on the inside is fearful to contemplate. Before he had passed his cap all the way round a ship officer came along and John did a quick disappearing act over the side.

Descending the ship ladder we boarded a river tug that took us up the river eighteen miles to Shanghai. On the way we passed many Chinese junks, high in bow and stern, low amidship, their red or brown square sails crossbarred with bamboo poles. A huge eye is always painted on each side of Chinese boats, for, as they say: "Junk no have eye, no can see, no can see, no can sabe, no can sabe, no can go."

As we neared Shanghai, smoke stacks, factories and ship-yards could be seen giving evidence of the modernization of China. When we reached the landing stage and took carriages and drove along the bund to "The Astor House" we realized we were in an important commercial metropolis of the European kind. On the left were substantial stone business blocks four or five stories high, while on the right was a pretty park sloping to the river which was swarming with steamers, junks and small boats.

The street was thronged. In and out among the carriages of the Europeans passed a multitude of Asiatics. Repulsive, ragged and indescribably dirty, most of them were. Coolies trotted along drawing the adopted Japanese rikisha; others were carrying immense weights balanced on poles; while others trundled the national conveyance, the wheelbarrow.

This barrow has a large wheel with a bench on each side for passengers or freight. The most surprising burdens are carried on this vehicle. It is not unusual to see a perspiring, mud-bespattered coolie staggering along with four fat and sleek Chinamen on his vehicle. Sometimes the whole family will be along. "Mommer" on one side in a purple silk coat, her small feet in pale blue satin slippers peeping out from dark blue bifurcated skirts, and her black hair correctly glued into puffs and wings; while with her arms which are adorned with jade bracelets, she holds her moon-faced offspring from falling into the mud. On the opposite side will be "Popper" and the rest of the family, with the marketing of vegetables, pigs and fowls, dead or alive.

The natives of northern China are large, well built and muscular. The Chinamen in America are the small men of southern China, and nearly all from the one city of Canton.

European Shanghai has been built within the last sixty years on land granted as a concession to foreign nations for commercial purposes outside the Chinese city. The English and French have their own sections, their own police, and courts.

The English "bobby" looks as though he had just stepped out of the Strand. The Chinese officer's uniform is a compromise. The middle part is in European style, but he wears Chinese boots and a funnel-shaped tin hat with a tassel. The Indian police are the most picturesque. They are tall and slender, and at the top they have eighteen inches or more of turkey red turban, wonderfully and fearfully made. They also have good durable complexions, dreamy brown eyes and fierce black whiskers carefully parted in the middle.

After several efforts we secured a guide who knew at one and at the same time something of English and something of the town. We then invaded the old walled city of the Chinese quarter. As soon as we penetrated the tunnel-like gateway we realized we were in the real China. On each side lay beggars, derelicts of humanity, in every stage of deformity and distress. As we traversed the streets, many of which are only four feet wide, in which the sun cannot penetrate, we remembered the Japanese remark, "The Chinese are the dirtiest people in the world except the Russians."

We passed the open booths of the jade cutters, and comb makers. Then the guide plunged through a dark passage, and we followed single file, Chinese fashion, through crooked corridors and alleys misty with the weight of the forty-seven original stinks, and emerged into an open court.

Here were arranged in rows earthen caldrons containing water in various stages of green stagnation in which were swimming Chinese gold fish in assorted sizes, and various styles. Each fish had several tails of flowing pink chiffon with ruffles around the borders caught up at the sides with red fins. When they swam across the tank their gauzy tails trailed out behind in a way that was "just too lovely for anything," as the dress-makers would say.

Guide said, "Suppose Mellican man likee put clean water? Then kille fish; China fish no likee clean water."

"Must be the same with the men," the Philosopher remarked. "Cleanliness might kill them, but if dirt gives health they'll never die."

We passed on traversing a street bordered on one side by shops and restaurants, and on the other by what might at one time have been a small canal, but which was nearly filled with slimy filth on the surface of which meandered a tiny stream that was liquid enough to flow. Every stone in the street was slippery and sodden with ooze, and the stench, the awful stench! Oh, that a kind providence, in pity and charity, had granted us a cold in China. The memory of it lingers, but not by request.

The "Odors of Cathay" at their best are sandal wood, burning punk, and opium; but alas, there are other odors peculiarly Chinese before which the strongest English language is as helpless as the prattle of an infant. They combine into a terrifying aggregation of stinks, to which Perfume de Polecat would be as Attar of Roses.

At last we reached the celebrated Mandarin Gardens, and passing through an elaborate stucco archway, found ourselves standing by a lily pond with banks of grass and flowers. It was a relief. We filled our lungs with the fresh air and looked about.

The Garden is enclosed by a wall supporting the elongated and undulated body of a
dragon. Its terra cotta head is reared in
terrifying ferocity at one side of the gateway, while its body encircles the garden, and
its tail is warningly uplifted at the other side
of the gate. Its body is formed of half circles of terra cotta roof tiles laid with the
convexity upward, each tier resting its edges
on the tops of the curves of the tiles beneath;
an arrangement which gives the effect of
scales to this uncanny creature.

In the few acres enclosed by this wall are
all the types of rustic scenery. There are
ranges of mountains fifty feet high with pagodas on their summits where one can drink
tea. There are cool caves, and shady nooks,
and tiny brooks with crescent bridges.

There is a little lake bordered by willow
trees, and in its center is a many-gabled, two
storied pagoda supported on posts. A zigzag
walk, also supported by posts, leads to it,
and on it stood Chinese women looking at
the lilies. The picture seemed strangely
familiar. Where had I seen it before? Ah,
yes! the plates, the old blue willow-pattern
ware! The picture might have stepped off
my Grandmother's platter.

In the afternoon we drove out the Bubbling Well Road, and through the European concession, and found it clean and unasiatic. In a Chinese garden we had tea and confections, and saw a native theatrical performance. This consisted of a deafening clash of cymbals, a rattle of wooden clappers, and an unearthly shrieking of Chinese fiddles, and a tiresome, lazy dance by children in spangled garments, and old men's masks.

We observed that at each place where a fee was required there was a terrific war of words between our guide, and the doorkeeper. We learned it was about the amount of extra "squeeze" which the doorkeeper was to collect from us, and the commission which he should pay our guide. China is the land of "squeeze," and such transactions are only the regular routine of business. After a particularly violent wordy battle with a gate keeper, which resulted in the guide reluctantly parting with one of the two Mexican dollars, which he had extorted from us, he angrily declared, "Chinaman heap big fool; him catchee one dollar,—wanchee two; him catchee two dollar,—wanchee four."

CHAPTER XIII.

HONG KONG.

We sailed down the China Sea in a calm. The China Sea is not always calm. There had been a shipwreck not long before, and when we passed the region where it occurred the Chinese, of whom there were hundreds in the steerage, held some sort of a religious ceremony. They burned reams of red paper on which prayers were written, and threw them burning overboard to be scattered by the wind. Various foods were thrown into the sea. By this means they appeased the dragons of the air, and honored the spirits of their countrymen who had perished in the shipwreck.

On the third morning we steamed up the channel with the rugged island of Hong Kong on the left and the rocky Chinese mainland on the right, and anchored in the harbor of Hong Kong. About us were war ships and merchantmen of many nations, for this, the best harbor of Asia is foremost in the amount of shipping, and one of the busiest ports in the world.

The city is hung on a steep hillside which gets steeper and steeper until it reaches the rocky "Peak" eighteen hundred feet high. Up this incline runs a cable road to the observatory and signal station at the top. In Hong Kong the social status corresponds with the altitude. "High Society" occupies the pretentious bungalows surrounded by spacious grounds on the upper roads and terraces, while "Low Society" crowds the slums at the water front. As people ·become richer they move higher.

The buildings are of stone with arcades on each floor to temper the heat which even in winter is extreme, at least in the sun.

Rikisha rides on the fine macadamized drives which belt the hill on three different levels are very interesting. One of these roads is constructed over the main canal of the water work system. Bordering the roads are charming villas perched on dizzy eminences, or embowered among tropical shrubs and flowering plants.

A ride up the cable inclined road is, to say the least, elevating. As the car ascends a panorama of city, harbor and shipping is spread before, or rather behind, like a scroll unrolled. It is like going up in a captive balloon.

Burning Prayers in the China Sea.

It is only about seventy years since the island became a British colony. During that time the English have done much for Hong Kong, but Hong Kong has done much more for the English, forming as it does the keystone of their arch of trade and influence in the far East. There is a rapidly increasing trade with the Philippines, and now that the Americans have dropped an oar into the Eastern Sea the Yankees of Manila feel quite neighborly with the Britishers of Hong Kong.

CHAPTER XIV.

CANTON AND THE CANTONESE.

By taking the evening boat from Hong Kong one may reach Canton early the next morning. The voyage up the bay in the balmy air and sunset glow of Southern China is a voyage long to be remembered. When, at length, the lights have faded in the west, and the timid stars peep out from the purple of the heavenly vault, and the darkening shadows of evening permit only the horizon line to mark itself against the sky, there arises another light, more mysterious, more weird, and more fascinating. Flecks of pale blue light cap the breaking crests of the steamer's wash and glimmer in the wake. The ruffling waves that break from the prow flash into fire, and outline the dark hull of the ship in a glowing frame. This is the phosphorescent sea.

The next morning at day-break we were awakened by a chattering like a thousand magpies. The boat was moored to the dock at Canton and myriads of Chinese were in view. The dock swarmed with them.

The river was crowded with their boats. We went ashore, mounted sedan chairs, and were carried by coolies to the hotel on Shameen Island, the foreign concession on which are located the European consulates, residences and hotels. This island is connected with the native city by a bridge protected with massive fortified gates and guarded by soldiers.

After breakfast we began our two days' sight seeing. Coolie chairs afford the only means of rapid transit in Canton. Journeys about the city are not long, for the population of nearly two millions is crowded into an area of only two miles by four. The streets are perhaps ten feet wide. The buildings are two to five stories high. The narrow chink of sky that otherwise would be visible is obscured by innumerable awnings, and black signs painted with red or gold characters hanging across the street; and by all manner of laundries and sundries hanging from the windows. Chairs must be carried single file, and turning can only be done at the street crossings. The streets are cleaner and odors less athletic than in Shanghai, although if I had seen Canton first I would not have believed a dirtier place could exist.

The shops are open to the street and all kinds of queer foods are exposed for sale. All manner of strange fish, birds, beasts and reptiles seem to be represented, trussed on sticks, dried, smoked and apparently varnished. I saw several small animals in that condition, and from their very long tails by which they were hung up, I concluded they were not rabbits.

It is a short ride to the Examination Hall. China is the originator of the State examination system. Practically all Chinese are eligible to enter these examinations. Philosophy and literature are the principal subjects. On passing the lower grades one becomes eligible for minor political positions. If he desires higher appointment he may enter higher examinations, and if he passes the highest examination he becomes eligible for appointment as Mandarin of the first class or even for Viceroy. These examinations are said to be impartially conducted by government officials.

One would not suspect the destiny of the most populous empire in the world could be influenced by such an unprepossessing institution. After passing an entrance gate we crossed a barren court populated by pigs,

The Examination Hall.

dogs and children equally dirty. We passed up a stone walk covered with a roof of translucent sea shells to a central temple stacked with boards used in making seats and tables required in the examinations. From this temple, walks lead to the twelve thousand individual cells in which the students are locked for the two days and nights allotted for the completion of their essays or poems; for the examinations are on literature and not on the sciences. These cells are only about five and one-half by four feet—rather cramped quarters in which to spend forty-eight continuous hours, for an American, but a whole recreation park for the over-crowded Cantonese.

One of the curious temples we visited is known by the cheerful name of the "Temple of Horrors" because in side-chapels are depicted the different varieties of punishment to be expected in the Chinese Hell. It was much like the chamber of horrors in the "Eden Musee" in New York or "The Wax Works" in London. The figures are in wax, life size, and vividly painted. They are supposed to frighten the people into being very, very good. Among the tortures represented are unhappy Chinamen being boiled in oil, sawed between boards and crushed under a bell. The one who was being skinned alive was perhaps guilty of grafting. This is a popular temple on account of its many devils. The Chinese pantheon is composed of numerous devils, and they are all bad. If there are any good devils, they are shamefully neglected, for the Chinese cannot understand why good Joss sticks and fire-crackers should be wasted on a God who would not harm them.

The court-yard is well occupied by fortune tellers, who will tell you "welly good luck fortune welly, welly cheap," but for a little more they will tell you something important that you "really should know." The way they jerk aside the curtain of the future is by burning strips of gilt, or silvered paper, and observing how the ashes fall. Of course "money must cross the palm" before the charms will work. I believe this is true of the cult in all countries.

As we proceeded through the narrow streets our carriers gave warning of our approach by peculiar cries. Foot travelers and coolies carrying burdens flattened themselves against the walls to make room for the "foreign devils." But there came a time when the clash of gongs approaching caused our guide to reverse the order. Our little caravan halted and the carriers crowded our chairs against the wall. A great Mandarin was approaching and he must have the right of way. We straightened ourselves in our chairs, and full of expectancy, awaited the great man. The clash of brass drew nearer and there appeared between the rows of celestials that lined the walls a most ridiculous retinue.

When a Mandarin travels it must be with great pomp, surrounded by his servants and armed retainers, but such a large retinue costs money even in China; so instead of keeping the men he keeps their uniforms and when he wishes to travel across the city sends his servants into the streets to impress into his service any vagabonds on whom violent hands may be laid. This "round up" was a sorry looking lot. There were perhaps fifteen in the straggling procession and three or four uniforms did duty in sections for the entire army.

First came a man, resplendent in a red cotton jacket, carrying a red banner with black characters announcing the name and degrees of the approaching dignitary. Then came a coolie in a pagoda hat tied on with his queue. He was industriously clashing large brass cymbals. Behind him came another belaboring a tom-tom with all his might. Then came a fellow wearing the remainder of the leading man's uniform. He carried aloft a mighty two-storied, red cotton umbrella. Then came the regular infantry consisting of two men carrying rusty flint-lock muskets. Thus preceded, came the chair of his highness, the Mandarin,—solemn, dignified and owlish in immense round goggles, green plush jacket and cone-shaped hat with a big tassel bobbing from the top. Behind him came the cavalry consisting of two men on shaggy ponies, and last of all came the artillery in the person of a coolie staggering under the weight of an enormous flint-lock musket which must have been twelve feet long. It was rusty and dusty and the hammer was tied on with a conspicuous bit of Manilla rope.

The procession having passed, we proceeded on our way through Jade Street and Ivory Carving Street to the Flowery Pagoda. Pagodas are the only characteristic monuments of Southern China. This one is familiar to every school boy, for it adorns the first page of the chapter on Asia in the geography, along with the elephant of India, and the junks of Japan.

No Canton guide will permit his tourist to escape seeing the execution grounds and the prisons. They possess a gruesome interest. The execution ground is about the size of a dozen city lots, and is usually occupied by fresh pottery in the process of drying. When wanted for official purposes the pottery is hurried away.

Criminals condemned to die do not know when will be the time of their execution. They are confined together in a pen and may be called at an time. Every Mandarin, or Judge, must witness the carrying out of his own capital sentences. Whenever he thinks it a good day for executions he travels to the grounds with his terrifying procession, and Hip Hop the Highbinder, or Ping Pong the Pirate, or some other criminal is ordered to be brought before him.

From the nearby prison the culprit is carried securely trussed and safely crated in a wicker cage. He is made to kneel. An assistant holds his head by the queue, while the Lord High Executioner does the rest with his trusty snicker-snee. The old executioner

showed us the official sword used in thousands of executions. He called to the curious street crowd that had followed us, that
he would cut some one's head off to show the
foreigners how it was done, whereupon the
crowd fled in a panic. Their terror and
precipitate exit seemed such a good joke to
the old executioner that he chuckled in
ghoulish glee. We consequently saw no execution, but there were plenty of fresh heads
on exhibition. Nearby is the cross-on which
the cruel sentence of cutting in a thousand
pieces is executed as an extreme punishment.

In the adjoining jail prisoners are herded
in pens. Some are loaded with chains, some
locked in wooden boxes so small that they
cannot stand or straighten their legs, and
some were undergoing the punishment of the
cangue. This is a wooden collar of two inch
plank about three feet square. When it is
locked on, the wearer cannot lie down, nor
brush from his face the flies and vermin with
which the jail abounds, nor even feed himself. If friends from outside or other prisoners do not place food in his mouth he
will starve. Very few survive the punishment of the cangue over three months. The
prisoners seemed to bear their suffering with

stoical indifference and some even with grinning cheerfulness.

We were glad to escape the gruesome sights and return to the European atmosphere of the hotel on Shameen Island.

CHAPTER XV.

THE FLOWER BOATS—CHINESE PUBLIC
OPINION.

In the evening in the company of an English gentleman, long a resident of Canton, we visited the flower boats. The flower boats are a sort of Cantonese Coney Island. There the gilded youths and giddy old boys of Canton disport themselves with whatever is the Chinese equivalent for wine, women and song. In this case it appeared to be opium, fan tan, and chop suey. These boats are chained together and visitors walk from one to the other to see the different forms of Chinese gaiety, such as music halls, restaurants, opium dens, gambling establishments and tea houses. The only dissipation we indulged in was tea and sweetmeats served by Chinese maidens, whose smoothly-oiled raven tresses were done up in a pad over the right ear and ornamented with wonderful hair pins with silk and tinsel tassels. The furnishings were gaudy but there was a substantial tone added by the heavy black teak wood, carved furniture and walls inlaid with mother-of-pearl. The musicians, or rather the noisicians, were ever present. The beat of the tom-tom, the squeak of the one-stringed fiddle, and the shriek of the bamboo fife, rent our ears and wounded our musical sensibilities.

In another tea house we had an unexpected pleasure. Our English friend accidentally met a Chinese diplomat of his acquaintance. He was a man of considerable importance whose name is so top-heavy with fame it would not do to mention it here. Our friend cautioned us not to offer to shake hands when we were introduced but to follow the Chinese custom of salutation.

We were introduced in Chinese and of course did not understand a word our friend was saying about us, but the Chinaman who was robed in resplendent silks smiled like a seraph, bowed low, and with his right hand seized his left hand and shook it cordially. We did the same. Through an interpreter he said:

"I am always glad to meet foreigners and am very sorry I cannot speak English. I am now too old to learn a language, but my sons speak English and French. I have three sons and they are all in Europe being educated. You know China is old but there is a new China arising."

At his order, there had been placed before us on the teak wood table bowls of tea covered with saucers, but which according to the Chinese etiquette were not to be drunk until the termination of the interview. He explained the many varieties of the tea enumerated on the menu card, some of which were very rare, expensive and never exported, and then he inquired: ·

"Do you enjoy our music?"

Our English friend came to our rescue in this dilemma and admitted there was some disagreement on the subject. Of course there was not, for we were unanimous in the opinion that it is a nerve-racking discord.

"It is not strange you do not appreciate it," said the diplomat in the sing song intonation of the Chinese language. "China was the first to compose and write music and had musical conservatories while the people of Europe were still chasing rabbits in the stone age. We have the advantage of several thousands of years of musical culture. What sounds to you a discord is to us the sweetest harmony. I am told that in America and Europe people who are uneducated in

music prefer simple tunes and primary har-
monies to the grand music of Wagner. Musical culture is necessary to appreciate your
grand opera and classical music, but you
must be educated still further before you can
be expected to arrive at the Chinese type of
music."

This explanation nearly killed the Philosopher. With such a yellow-music peril
confronting us, he advocated prohibition of
musical conservatories, and high license on
country singing classes.

The diplomat smiled at us through his
round glasses and asked:

"Have you been well treated in China?"

"Oh yes." In that we were also unanimous. "We have been very well treated indeed;" and then he put us to shame. There
was sadness and reproach in his voice as he
replied:

"I am glad to hear it. Chinese gentlemen
who travel to America do not receive the
same courtesy. They are taken from their
first-class accommodations and thrown into
vile prisons at immigration stations to await
the red tape of diplomatic intervention.
The sons of our Mandarins, traveling for
pleasure and education, have been treated as

coolie laborers and sent to detention pens. We are the only people which you discriminate against on account of their nationality, and yet what immigrants do you admit that are more law abiding, honest and hard working than the Chinese? We men of China consider that unfair, and since we do not have the might to force from you the rights you grant to other nations we can only resort to commercial warfare, the boycott. We bear no malice to you as individuals, and shall continue to treat all foreigners with kindness, or indifference, but we will try to get along without your cotton, your machinery, your pocket knives with six blades and a cork screw, your music boxes, your whiskey and other agents of civilization."

The Philosopher inquired, "Do you approve of our missionaries, and their work in China?"

"I have a high regard for the missionaries personally, and for their schools and hospitals, but the Chinese would prefer to go to their own heaven in their own way. Suppose they should have the same experience when they reach the American heaven that they have when they reach an American port. You exclude us from your country on earth, why do you insist on driving us into your heaven? Will our company be more agreeable there?" And he smiled again.

We assured the diplomat that he had given us food for thought, and drinking our tea we arose. There was more bowing and smiling and shaking of our own hands; then we returned to our boat. As we were being rowed back to our hotel, the Philosopher admitted that this Chinese puzzle is still far from being solved.

CHAPTER XVI.

THE TEMPLE OF HONAN—HOW THE DEVILS ARE IMPOSED UPON.

On the following day we visited among other places, the temple of Five and Five Hundred Genii where we saw an image of Marco Polo, in company with those of the five hundred wise disciples of Buddha—rather a distinguished honor to be given the early Italian navigator.

We reached the famous temple of Honan in time to be present at a Buddhist religious service. It was strikingly like the Christian service. Kneeling worshippers responded in unison to the intonations of the priests in flowing yellow robes, who bowed before the figure of Buddha; there was burning incense, and solemn music. Nothing was missing, not even the collection.

We made the rounds of the monastery, which is one of the largest in Southern China. We saw the immense caldron where rice is cooked for thousands, and the hollow log on which the cook beats a tattoo to call the priests, who come with their bowls to receive their rations.

We were shown the sacred hogs, who devour the food the devout people dedicate to the Gods, that is, they do if the priests give them a chance. These hogs appeared contented, and meditative, but not forgetful of the trough, as is becoming their station, and the certain knowledge that theirs is a life appointment, and that when they die, they will be decently buried with proper ceremony.

The priest who guided us did not seem so near Nirvana as his porcine associates, for he lusted strongly, after the carnal gratification of tobacco, in fact he reminded us of his desire several times, and finally with success.

As we were being carried back to the hotel, the evening burning of Joss sticks was progressing before each shop. The air was heavy with smoke, and vibrant with the rattle of exploding fire-crackers. In a niche by the entrance to each building, or shop, stands the family altar with its lamp ever burning for the honor of the ancestors, and the protection of the house against the ever present malevolent spirits of the air. These devils are to be appeased by various bribes of money, gold, silver, and food, and frightened by Joss sticks, and fire-crackers. But, alas, the commercial spirit of the Chinese extends even into their religion, for spurious money, gold and silver made of gilt paper and tinsel, is burned before the altars, and the food offered to the Gods they take back and eat.

When we were safely taking our ease on the hotel veranda in the foreign concession, we heard the seven o'clock gun, and the beating of the tom-toms, announcing the closing of the outer wall gates, and the inner gates that subdivide the city into wards.

While the ways of John Chinaman seem strange to us we should remember that our ways are are equally strange to him, and perhaps equally abhorent. It is more difficult to place ourself at the viewpoint of others than it is to write a book about it.

> " O, wad the powers some giftie gie us
> To see oursel's as ithers see us."

The following letter written by a Chinese tourist traveling for pleasure in America, gives the Chinese view of our flaunted superior civilization.

"WALDORF ASTORIA HOTEL, N. Y.

DEAR CHIN CHIN :

America is a most barbaric country. The men do not shave their heads, ears, or eyelids. They eat meat half raw, still dripping blood, tearing it apart by means of iron tools. They cannot use chop sticks and can only afford rice once a week.

They have scarcely any respect for their ancestors and the way they treat their women is simply shocking. They take them out to what they call " Balls " with scarcely any clothing on the upper part of their bodies, it having mostly slipped down so it drags behind, and there to simply hellish noise, which they call music, they wrestle their women all over the floor until they are exhausted.

Yours indignantly,

CHOP SUEY."

CHAPTER XVII.

THE EDUCATION OF CHINA.

Confucianism is the leading religion of China. It is a system of philosophy, ethics and morals founded by Confucius about five hundred years before Christ and a hundred years after Buddhism was founded in India. Its five basic precepts are: fidelity to the reigning authority; reverence for parents; submission of the wife to the husband; obedience of younger sons and daughters to the oldest son; and the duties of man to man, which last is summed up in their golden rule, "Do not do unto others as you would not have them do unto you." One of his five hundred disciples taught that good should be returned for evil, but Confucius rebuked him saying, "What then will you return for good? Recompense injury with *justice*, and return good for good."

Whether these teachings have anything to do with it or not, it is a fact that the Chinese merchant is considered absolutely reliable and honest in all business transactions.

When a Chinese merchant says "Can do" after a verbal agreement, the European trader
knows it will be done even if the Chinaman
loses money. He drives a close bargain, but
when the "Can do" is passed, his word will
be kept. There are no bankruptcies. Debts
do not outlaw. A failure would be a serious
calamity, for the entire family would be held
liable and probably heads would fall.

As we steamed down the Pearl River the
next day, returning to Hong Kong, we
passed some very pretty hill scenery. We
observed that the forts China has constructed to control the river are no trifling affairs.
Perhaps China will some day be able to kill
her thousands like Japan and become recognized as civilized.

In the meantime China is dreadfully
heathen. But there is hope. We are edu-
cating her. Our churches contribute millions in money and hundreds of precious lives
of missionaries to teach the Chinamen that
their religion is all wrong, and their civilization away behind the times and not suited to
them at all. If the Chinamen offer any ob-
jection, or throw any stones, or break any
windows, or chase the unwelcome teacher
of a strange religion out of their neighbor-

hood, the cable gets hot with the calls for gunboats. The lion roars, and the eagle screams. Then the war ships and soldiers come and take a province or two; force the helpless government to sign a treaty that the province is gladly given up, sold, leased, or given away; that they love the missionaries dearly, that they are very, very sorry their property or feelings were hurt; and, that they will cut off the head of somebody, and see that it does not occur again.

But they are learning. They are learning how to build forts and train men, and borrow money, and manufacture rifles and big guns. In due course of time they will become civilized, and have an army of a hundred million men; then, perhaps, an Asiatic Napoleon, another Mongol like Genghis Kahn who conquered Central Asia in the thirteenth century will rise up among them, who knows how to handle such an army because he has been educated at the expense of the American people at West Point, and— then may all the world tremble.

On the way down the river we passed a large house-boat flying the American flag. It was floating lazily at anchor near the bank. Its decks were shaded by awnings and comfortable with hammocks and steamer chairs. It looked very cool and luxurious. Its occupants waved us a cheery salutation as we passed. The captain replied:

"No that is not an American millionaire but missionaries spending a season on the river for the good of the natives.

The captain was a hardened sailor. He appeared to believe that the foreign teachers destroyed the natives' reverence for the moral code of their ancestors without supplying them with a working quantity of the Christian conscience.

He related a story of the missionary house-boat, which illustrates the patience required to awaken China.

The missionary's class having assembled the good man proceeded to throw the light into dark places in this manner:

"Who made you?" he asked of the China boy at the end of the line.

"Ancestors."

"No. God made you," corrected the missionary. "Now who made you?"

"God."

"Correct. Now what did he make you of?"

"Spirits," replied heathen number two.

"No," corrected the missionary again. "He made you of dirt. Now what did He make you of?"

"Dirt."

"Correct. Now what did he command you not to do?"

"Confucius, him say, no makee ancestor losee face; no stealee, no talkee lie," promptly answered number three.

"The answer is 'sin,'" sternly corrected the missionary. "Now what did God command you not to commit?"

"Sin."

"Now what is the Trinity?"

On this the Chinaman figured some time and finally declared. "One is three and three is one, Chinaman no can do." This required a long explanation and in the meantime convert number two disappeared.

"Now we will review the lesson," said the missionary.

"Now, number one, who made you?"

"God."

"What did he make you of?"

"Sin," came the surprising admission from convert number three.

"Oh my, no!"

"Yes, me catche 'sin.' Dirtee Chinaman,

him jump overboard, takee washee. Him talkee plenty good Englis, catchee job guide; him no more likee Melican Joss."

CHAPTER XVIII.

MACAO, THE MONTE CARLO OF THE EASTERN SEA.

Macao is picturesque. As our steamer approached there was a suggestion of a water color sketch in its buildings, tinted pale blue, salmon or gleaming white, which terraced the rugged peninsula in an azure sea. It was built by the Portuguese four hundred years ago, and looks its age.

The mob of Chinese rikisha men at the dock were held in check by a pompous little Portuguese policeman. He was less than five feet in height and weighed perhaps a hundred pounds. He carried a pistol and an enormous saber. His black eyes flashed from under bushy eyebrows, and his exuberant whiskers bristled with importance. He did not hesitate to slap the Chinamen in the face, and if one showed the slightest resentment, he would get a resounding whack with the flat of the saber across his solar plexus, or on his ultimate if he had turned to flee.

When we had at last selected rikishas we made fast time to the Boa Vista Hotel. The view from the porches was of such striking beauty that it brought rhapsodies of delight from every tourist. The hotel was on a hillside at one end of a crescent bay. At the other end was a cone shaped hill crowned by the Montee fortress. On the glassy surface of the bay floated junks and the bat-winged boats of the fishermen. Facing the bay is the Praya Grande, a wide esplanade, thronged with promenaders. It is shaded by banyan trees, and protected from the sea by a substantial granite wall. At the further end of the Praya Grande are the public gardens beautifully laid out and glowing with tropical flowers. A military band was playing there, and the sweet strains of music mellowed by distance, were brought us on the fragrant breezes. Macao might be called an Asiatic Naples, but, on account of its many gambling establishments it is known as the Monte Carlo of the Eastern Sea.

In the evening we went to one of the brilliantly lighted gambling houses to see the popular game of Fan-tan. We were shown to a balcony from which we could look down upon a fan-tan table, around

which was a crowd of Chinamen, Portuguese, and Eurasians. High class natives
and foreigners use this upper balcony when
they play. A dealer for the house sits at a
large table upon which are painted four
squares marked 1, 2, 3 and 4. A pile of copper
coins is before him. He pushes a handful
towards the center of the table, and partially covers it with a bowl. Then the betting
begins. The players can place their money
on either of these four numbers. When the
bets are placed, the dealer lifts the bowl and
counts the coins back into his pile in lots of
four, using a chop stick that all may see the
counting. There will be left over an odd 1,
2, or 3 coins, or they will come out even on
the 4. The number left over wins, and all
who have their money on that square are
paid three times their bet, less ten per cent.
commission. All others lose to the house.
An attendant on the balcony attended to the
players, lowering their money to the table
and drawing it up by means of a cord and
basket. The bets were usually silver coins,
but sometimes large bank notes traveled
down, and fat rolls came up, by the cord and
basket route. It is purely a game of chance,
and quite exciting.

The house served tea and nuts. A few Chinamen were smoking opium on the teak wood divans around the gallery, or dozing quietly in the opium fiend's paradise.

On our return to the hotel, how charming were the cool verandas! The street lights of the Praya Grande outlined the crescent of the bay, and from the distant public garden came the soft strains of a waltz. Across the dark waters of the bay stretched a shimmering pathway of silver to the low hanging moon.

The next day we visited the picturesque ruins of the old cathedral at the top of a long flight of steps. It is interesting from the fact that immense treasure is supposed to be buried in the neighborhood, and that many Japanese converts who escaped the persecution in Japan, assisted in its building.

Nearby is the entrance to Camoens' Gardens where the exiled soldier-poet of Portugal completed his heroic epic "The Lusiadas." Through a mediaeval gateway we entered a garden blooming with many flowers. The air was sweet with heliotrope, lavender, and rose. We passed an imposing old mansion occupied by the military Governor, and walked down an avenue in the cooling shade of the spreading banyan trees, then up a small hill, and found ourselves in a little nook shaded by immense overhanging boulders. This is the grotto of the Camoens, the spot where the immortal bard retired to receive inspiration to write the greatest epic poem in Portuguese literature for the glory of Louis of Portugal, who had exiled him, because he knew too much, and wrote too truly.

In an archway formed by the boulders are verses in various languages praising Camoens. One in English began:

> "Gem of the Orient, Earth, and open Sea,
> Macao; that on thy lap and on thy breast
> Has gathered beauties all the loveliest
> Which the sun shines on in his majesty."

There was more of this poem, but as it progressed it got worse, so I divide it in the middle, and deliver only the top.

CHAPTER XIX.

SINGAPORE.

On the voyage down from Hong Kong ducks came out; also lawns, and pongees. It was hot, and the dark man who pulled the punka was overworked. The punka is an early ancestor of the electric fan. If he pulled too lazily at the rope the wrath of some officer was sure to fall upon him. This particular punka oscillated over the table in the dining cabin, and faintly stirred the humid air into the semblance of a breeze. Sometimes he held the cord with his toes, and then the upper part of him slept, but his leg was awake and swung regularly back and forth pulling the cord.

At Singapore we were within a few degrees of the equator, and here we stopped for a day. A drive to the Botanical Gardens was full of interest. The glare of the chalk roads was relieved by the dense green of the tropical foliage. The bungalows of the European residents are raised on stilts to permit the breezes to temper the heat and incidentally, perhaps, to discourage the malaria germs, fever microbes, snakes, tigers and other dangers that are the principal sub-jects for afternoon conversations. In the town itself the malaria and fever germs are constant visitors, and boa constrictors and tigers occasionally call.

At the Zoological Garden there is a charming collection of snakes—a whole temperance lecture,—and several nice glossy tigers. There is also a cageful of monkeys thirsting for knowledge; one reached a surprisingly long arm through the bars and appropriated my glasses. He carried them to the highest perch, then he chuckled with delight and gravely looked through them. He was plainly surprised. His exclamations attracted a dozen other monkeys. They quarreled about my glasses, and then divided them, and when I came away one was parading the cage looking through a single eye-glass like Montmorency of the "Happy Hooligan" family.

The street scenes of Singapore are especially interesting. All the races of the East are represented, with the Malays predominating. These people are shady of skin, lathy of leg and not much given to clothes. Such as they have are in all the colors of the rainbow. These benighted heathen are still in darkness regarding the advantages of clothing in their hot climate, and they will not realize that it is very improper to go about clad only in red breech clouts and brass anklets. Occasionally some dandy among them will appear of a holiday carrying European clothes to extremes by wearing a discarded silk hat and patent leather shoes, but alas there will be no more in the middle than before.

Here we entered a Hindoo temple at the invitation of the good-natured Cerebus at the gate who wore a few clothes and a kindly smile. His teeth were dyed a deep crimson by the betel nut he was industriously chewing. He showed us several fierce idols and two cars of Juggernaut.

CHAPTER XX.

PENANG—TROPICAL FRUITS.

All day we sailed up the Strait of Malacca. Some of us slept on deck to catch a glimpse of the Southern Cross. Whether we saw it, is a matter of faith, and "faith is believing what you know ain't so," as the small boy said. We did, however, see the hills of Sumatra, and the mountains of the Malay Peninsula. One of the highest peaks is Mount Ophir, where, according to a tradition, the Queen of Sheba had gold mines.

The sea was serene and on its glassy surface the passing clouds were reflected. Frequently we saw driftwood. Once we passed a native canoe upturned. The breeze was fresh with the odor of the ocean and soft with the balm of the Indian Isles where:

> "Are still the heavy blossomed bowers,
> And the heavy fruited trees;
> The summer Isles of Eden
> In their purple sphere of seas."

There was a langorous charm in the air. To stretch in a steamer chair and give one's

Cars of Juggernaut.

self up to the happiness of indolence, was a
luxury which was all too soon interrupted by
our arrival at Penang.

Penang, where the nutmegs come from, is
much like Singapore. The people look even
more barbaric on account of the custom of
painting their foreheads, arms and bodies to
indicate their caste. It is very effective on
their brown skins. Another race, the Chet-
ties, shave the front of their scalps but allow
their back hair to fall over their shoulders.

We took garees, as the native carriages
are called, and drove some four miles to the
Botanical Garden. The road was through
groves of cocoanut, date and areca palms,
nutmeg, clove and cinnamon trees. We
passed many spacious European bungalows
and native palm huts.

The Botanical Garden is a revel of tropical luxuriance, strange flowers, wonderful
orchids and heavy perfumes. Back of the
garden rises a hill, billowy with the green of
tree tops. From a notch in its crest a mountain stream tumbles hundreds of feet in a
foaming cascade. In the sunlight it gleamed
like a white satin ribbon on a green velvet
curtain. We climbed to the cascade, ad-
mired its beauties, and filled our sun helmets

with brilliant flowers that nodded from the rocky clefts.

In the cooling sprays of the waterfall we tasted the fruit of the tropics. Our Malay boy opened the basket and presented a fruit that looked something like a yellow tomato. It was a mango. Its watery interior was held together by a fibrous, cottony network, and the eating of one is like unto the sucking of a sweet rag. Another fruit looked like a baked potato and tasted like a pear gone wrong. Then came the mangostine. This was a highly-ornamented fruit trimmed with four small leaves at its stem, and a mark on its tip like a marigold. We cut through its purple skin and its rose-tinted husk, and a snowy white heart separated. This readily broke into quarters like little blocks of ice cream. I tasted a portion and gave thanks; for it melted in the mouth with a cool, refreshing lemon-phosphate taste that would delight a Sybarite, whatever a Sybarite may be.

The sunset as seen from the ship when it steamed away from Penang that evening was strangely beautiful. The sun approached the distant hills in a glory of golden haze barred by burnished copper. The cloud margins faded into pale green and turquois, touched here and there with rose and amber. Into this riot of colors, streamers of pink from the sinking sun shot into the heavens in rays of radiating glory, changing constantly and suffusing all the circle of the horizon with rosy opalescence. It was one of those sunsets that not even fancy can tint; a fragment, perhaps, of the glory that surrounds the eternal throne.

The colors faded; the clouds darkened; only a dull red glow lingered on the western horizon. The heavenly vault deepened to azure; the tiny stars peeped shyly out; and a great, round, red moon slowly rose out of the glistening waters of the Indian Ocean.

CHAPTER XXI.

ARRIVAL AT COLOMBO AND A SAD DECEPTION.

As we approached Ceylon we could see the hazy blue mountains with puffs of steamy clouds hanging on their wooded slopes; and forests of palms fringing the sandy beaches where the white line of the breakers could be seen. Many passengers stood at the rail a long time sniffing the air, for the "spicy breezes that blow soft o'er Ceylon's Isle," but all they got for their trouble were sunburned noses from the reflection of the sun on the water.

When we came to anchor, numerous native boys in breech clouts paddled to the ship on rafts of three slender logs. Standing on these uncertain platforms they lifted up their voices in glad peans of joy, for money was coming their way. They sang "Ta-ra-ra-boom-de-aye," beating time by slapping their naked sides with their elbows. When passengers had been attracted to the rail, these unchins cried "Throw a penny, Mister?" When a coin was thrown into the water every urchin dived. Down they went, scrambling for the coin, and when they came up one of them was sure to have it between his teeth.

Some of the impatient passengers went ashore on catamarans. A catamaran is a rakish looking craft made of a hollow log. It is capable of sustaining a not too obese passenger in the center, and a lean native at either end. It would immediately capsize were it not for the outrigger, which consists of a small log lashed at the ends of two poles and floating alongside. This humble outrigger is an essential support of the boat. From this simple craft the Philosopher from Philadelphia deduced some comforting morals.

"It is sometimes given to the weaker half," he said, "to be the support of the strong," and he added sadly, "sometimes the sole support." "It also teaches the value of little things; for instance, if our salary is small we should be consoled by the thought that such as it is, we need it."

The Philosopher had other inexpensive wisdoms of the catamaran variety, but his audience had climbed overboard to the steam tender.

After passing through the custom house with that sense of burning shame that comes from having nothing to smuggle, we stepped into rikishas, and were soon rolling along the sea-shore road to the Galle Face Hotel.

What a pleasure it is to one who has been a long time on shipboard to feel himself again on the solid earth. With what relief one can fill the lungs with air that has the odors of growing grasses and blooming flowers.

The roads of Colombo are made of molasses colored soil, which has a habit of meandering through the air, and settling on any face that happens to be convenient. This produces some curious maps on the perspiring faces of the tourists, but on the natives it doesn't show.

As we rode, I remarked to Phil, the Philosopher from Philadelphia, the strange absence of men. The way women are downtrodden in this heathen island is certainly a sin. Reared as I was in a land where women are respected, and protected, it filled me with indignation to see women, lovely women, engaged in every sort of occupation. There were frail women carrying burdens; slender women with soulful eyes toiling in the roads; fat women whose skirts were badly stretched to get around, driving nails and

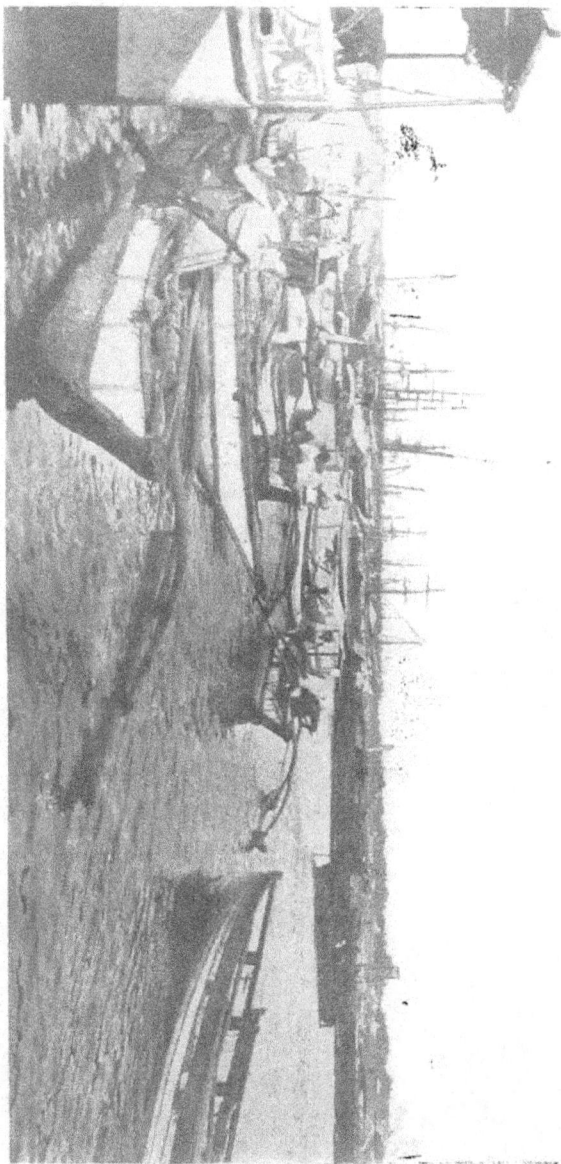

A Catamaran is a Rakish Craft.

hitting the heads every time; women driving bullock carts, and using frightful language; and women doing nothing, but throng the streets.

All of them wore skirts of checked calico tightly wrapped around their limbs, and their long hair was neatly done in top-knots, held by large tortoise shell combs.

Were there no men on the island? Apparently not. The Philosopher had read of some such island in the Southern Sea. Can this be the land of the Amazons? The Philosopher thought not, as he saw no spangled tights.

A beggar girl ran by my side. "Give me a penny," she said, tapping her forehead with one hand and rubbing her bare stomach with the other. "Give me a penny." Then she reversed the order, rubbing her forehead and tapping her stomach."*

"Give me a penny. You are my father."

"Impossible. I am a perfect stranger."

"You are my very good father," she insisted, salaaming as she ran. "You are my father; give me a penny." She kissed her hand and touched my white shoes.

"You are my father."

---

*A very difficult feat. Try it yourself.—*G. W. C.*

Here was a sad case. In all this town there was not a man to be her father. She must beg one. Anyone who had money would do. Not a man in sight but the Philosopher; and yet, it was curious, there were children,—many of them—I could recognize them anywhere. They wore no disguises. Clad in the rich brown tints of their complexions, and Trilby hearts, they stood forth in the perspective, living evidence of the needlessness of the masculine gender in the propagation of the species. I was dumbfounded. Here was a discovery. Beside it Darwin's discoveries and theories were as simple as nursery rhymes. It is true Prof. Loeb had discovered that sea urchins can be produced without male fertilization, but what was that compared to my discovery that land urchins can be produced without man. I would report it to the Scientific world at once, and emblazon my name high on the pinnacle of fame, beside Prof. Smitherene's whose paper on "Insomnia of the Industrious Flea" won the the Tanner's medal.

I bounded into the hotel, ordered a bale of paper and a quart of ink sent at once to my room and sprang up the stairs three steps at a time.

The Simple Life.

At last the writing material was brought—
by apparently another woman,—but, Shades
of Cleopatra! this one had whiskers.

"What," I said, a horrible suspicion chill-
ing my blood, "do you women wear whiskers
too?"

He turned reproachful eyes upon me and
sadly said:

"Master, I am the father of a family."

"But why these skirts; your Psyche knot;
your tortoise shell combs?" I inquired.

"'Tis the custom of my country," he replied calmly. "Shall I bring you tea?"

CHAPTER XXII.

IN AND ABOUT COLOMBO.

My room at the Galle Face Hotel over-
looked the ocean. Cocoanut trees waved
their fronds in front of the open windows,
and cast dark shadows in the evening when
the moonlight rippled on the sea.

I did not occupy my room alone. I shared
it with hordes of mosquitoes and red ants.
Netting around the bed kept the former at
bay, and one gets used to the latter.

My most frequent visitors were the crows.
They came early and stayed late. They sat
on the window ledge, and stared with their
heads tipped saucily to one side, and cawed
for the remains of Chota hadzri, or early
breakfast of toast and tea, which is brought
before one is out of bed according to the custom of the country.

One gradually gets accustomed to room
boys in skirts, Psyche knots, and hair combs.
With a little experience one can distinguish
the genuine female from the near-woman variety.

The women are highly ornamented with anklets, toe rings, finger rings, armlets, necklaces and ear-rings in curiously worked silver and gold, some set with native precious stones.   Even the nose is not spared.   Often a jeweled ornament is anchored in one side. Occasionally both sides of the nose are pierced, and hung with jeweled pendants. But men also wear much jewelry, consequently that is of little assistance in determining sex. It is safer, and better judgment to keep an eye out for whiskers.   Under seven years of age children are clothed only in jewelry, including a silver chain around the waist from which is suspended an ornament in the form of a Trilby heart in the location of the historical fig leaf.

The rides around Colombo are sources of ever-varying delight.   The roads wind through groves of cinnamon, nutmeg, clove and palm trees.   There is a depth of green that throws the purple of the passion flower and the scarlet of the hibiscus into brilliant relief.   The palm leaf cottages of the natives, half hidden in flowery bowers, the gracefully draped women, and the naked cherubs playing about, are in perfect harmony with the Orient of our dreams.

Wherever there is a pond or a river, one will generally find natives at their laundry work. They wash their clothes on themselves and take them off to dry in the wind. So skillful are they in exchanging their garments in public that at no time is too much bronze visible.

The natives wash the European's clothes by trailing them in the stream, and trashing a rock with them. This method is guaranteed to be the most destructive known, but these native laundries are among the most picturesque scenes in Ceylon.

One afternoon we drove to a Buddhist Temple, some miles out, where there is a large dagoba. A dagoba is a monument in somewhat the shape of a huge dinner bell, and usually contains some sacred relic or tomb. Far away in the tangled forest of the interior, are ruined cities, with dagobas three hundred feet high and four hundred feet in diameter at the base.

As it was a festival day we found the great court-yard gay with banners strung from masts. Natives were sitting in meditation under the sacred Bo tree. One of these trees stands in nearly every temple yard. It is considered the most desirable tree under

Under Seven.

which to meditate, because in its shade Buddha sat when he attained perfect sanctification.

A procession entered the grounds. At the head came a band of musicians with native instruments. Then followed young women draped in white, bearing on their heads urns containing rice and fruits as offerings for the support of the temple. Others bore trays of temple flowers, white and lily-like, with heavy perfume. The procession passed around the temple singing.

I opened my camera and prepared to take a picture. The action was observed, but I was not expelled. On the contrary two old gentlemen with patriarchal beards, who seemed to be the marshals of the occasion, offered to march the procession in any position I wished that I might get a good photograph. The festival was interrupted. The people marched and countermarched. Every suggestion was welcomed with the laughing good humor found in children and heathens. So much attention was embarrassing.

Finally my good patriarch friends asked if I would like to photograph the high priest. Of course I would, and would consider it a great honor. He said he would arrange it and disappeared.

Soon a chair was brought and placed at the temple entrance. The venerable priest came out and seated himself. The younger priests and temple attendants gathered around him. My two patriarch friends with the beards sat at his feet, and I took their photographs. The high priest did not speak English, but through an interpreter he wished us well, bowed profoundly, and withdrew within the temple.

Do you think a Cingalese traveling in America would meet with such courtesy if he should visit our churches during a festival?

With many bows and thanks we left our gentle heathen friends, the Buddhists. I am afraid I shall feel like a pious slanderer if in the little church at home I sing as the missionary plate is going round:

> " What tho' the spicy breezes
>   Blow soft o'er Ceylon's Isle,
> Where every prospect pleases
>   And ONLY MAN IS VILE."

Just as we reached the hotel a tropical storm overtook us. Black clouds rolled rapidly across the sky. The wind came roaring upon us, bending and shaking the palm trees like banners. The day suddenly became dark as twilight. Vivid lightnings slashed the

The Priests of the Temple Wore Yellow Robes Draped Like Roman Togas.

heavens, and thunder crashed a continuous cannonade. The rain fell in torrents. Presently the storm had passed. All was calm again and the sun shone brighter than before. It was like an outburst of passion that is followed by regret.

CHAPTER XXIII.

KANDY, AND THE KANDY TOOTH.

After a short railroad ride through a strange and interesting country, we arrived at Kandy, the ancient capital of the Cingalese Kings. Kandy is a charming place nestling among the hills on the border of· an artificial lake—one of the few remaining irrigation works of the ancient Kings who made Anuradhapura, the half-buried ancient city far away in the jungle, one of the most magnificent capitals of the world, rivaling Babylon and Nineveh in extent and splendor.

Near the center of the lake there is an island overgrown with palms and mossy trees. A palace was once there as beautiful as a poet's dream. It was the king's harem. Nothing now remains but a vine-covered arch. The king's gondola no longer touches the half buried marble stairs. The throb of the lute, the tinkle of the castanets, and the laughter of women, are no longer borne across the waters as they dance before the king. Now are heard only the songs of

They Marched Around the Holy of Holies.

birds, and the cooing of doves among the tangled vines.

The ancient Temple of the Tooth stands by the lake. This is one of the most revered spots in all Buddhism. It appears that when Buddha died he left a tooth which in after years became a bone of contention. During the quarrels of the Buddhists and Brahmins, it was deemed unsafe in India, and was brought to Ceylon in the third century, concealed in the hair of a princess. The devout king caused a shrine of gold and precious stones to be built for it. A thousand years later Indian invaders took the tooth, jewels and all, back to India; but it again found its way to Ceylon, and another shrine was built for it.

Last of all came the Portuguese, who were described by a writer of the time as "A race of men surpassingly white and beautiful, wearing boots and hats of iron, eating a white stone, and drinking blood, and having guns which would break a castle of marble."

The Portuguese landed and proceeded to rob the bodies and save the souls of the natives. They spread Christianity by fire and sword. They destroyed the temples; broke the irrigation dams; and carried the tooth of

Buddha to Goa, where the Archbishop in the presence of the Viceroy, publicly burned that sacred relic of a hundred million people.

But finally, in the course of time, the Portuguese were expelled by a just heaven,—and the Dutch.

The Dutch were more tolerant, being more concerned in getting business than saving souls; consequently a miracle was performed by which the late incinerated molar was materialized from thin air with nothing lost. In fact, those who have seen it say it is large enough for a horse.

However it may have been secured, it was duly incased in gold, placed in a jeweled casket, in a gold cabinet, in the Holy of Holies of the Temple of the Tooth in Kandy, and is accorded all the veneration of the original.

One morning we were aroused by the shrill notes of flutes, the banging of tom-toms and the shouts of a multitude. We hastily dressed and went out. A country delegation was passing to the temple bearing tribute of rice from the recent harvest. They were dressed in the gayest colors, and sang as they marched, two by two, in a long procession. The baskets of rice, bedecked

The Delegation was Holding a Religions Service and was Engaged in Prayer.

with temple flowers, were carried on the heads. There were many curious banners, and a canopy was carried over the procession.

We followed into the temple. A polite young priest secured for us an elevated position from which we were able to see and photograph the procession as it marched several times around the Holy of Holies which is a shrine built in the centre of the temple court-yard containing the sacred tooth. As they marched they sang and shouted "praises to Buddha," as the priest explained.

The young priest then showed us the treasures of the temple. He escorted us into a room dimly lighted with candles. Before an image of Buddha was a table loaded with temple flowers. The air was oppressive with their rich, sweet odor. He opened cabinets and showed us Buddhas in gold, in silver, and incrusted with precious stones. With evident pride, he opened another cabinet and exhibited a figure of Buddha fifteen inches high cut from a single rock crystal. This he said was a present from the King of Siam.

He took us to the library. This was an

upper floor of the turret-like corner of the
temple, and was nearly surrounded by an
arcade from which a splendid view of the
lake and hills could be obtained. We were
shown sacred tomes of the Buddhist scrip-
tures written by hand on palm leaves and
bound in golden covers incrusted with precious stones. He also showed with much respect a leaf from the original Bo tree in India, which is still alive, twenty-five hundred
years after Buddha sat in its shade. This
leaf was brought and presented by Sir Edwin
Arnold, author of "The Light of Asia,"
whose works are on the library shelves together with all the books in all languages
that have reference to the religion of Buddha.

We were then piloted through a crowd of
natives to the entrance of the shrine in the
yard. Up the sacred stairway the priest
made a way, crowding to one side the natives
who were devoutly crawling up on their
knees. These people scarcely noticed us.
Their lightly clasped hands, upturned eyes,
and rapt expressions indicated intense religious sincerity, and calm and earnest spirituality without hysteria. When we had
reached the top we found ourselves in a small

The Priests on a Platform Prayed Aloud Before the Kneeling Multitude.

room dimly lighted by candles, and packed
solid with natives. Beyond a railing, which
held back the crush of people, was a golden
pagoda-like casket, perhaps two feet high.
In this is the sacred tooth enclosed in several
smaller caskets. The tooth itself is shown only
on especially sacred occasions, much as the
sacred relics are shown in European cathedrals. We did not linger long. The air was too
redolent of perfumes, piety and perspiration.

On regaining the court-yard we found our
friends of the morning procession engaged
in a religious service. The priest secured for
us a position on the platform which surrounded the court from which we could get a good
view and photograph of the priests on one side,
and the assembled multitude on the other.
The priests were gathered on the platform
near a corner of the court. An old priest,
his strong, kind face uplifted to the heavens,
was repeating a service with the intonations
and mannerisms of our own clergy. The
people kneeling in the court-yard responded
in unison, bowing their heads and uplifting
their clasped hands at certain sentences. The
similarity to our Christian service was remarkable.

One evening we were entertained by the

Devil Dancers. The devils of disease and misfortune are supposed to be frightened away by their antics. At ten o'clock a company of nine men with attendants carrying torches came from the hills. There were six men with barrel drums, small drums and cymbals and three dancers. The dancers were loaded with silver bells and fantastic ornaments, which jingled as they marched up the street.

When this grotesque procession reached the open space before the hotel porch, where the spectators were congregated, they began a weird chant in nasal falsetto to the accompaniment of their strange musical instruments. Gradually their fervor increased and they began to strike the earth with their bare feet. The music became faster and faster and their steps more sprightly until they bounded about in wild acrobatic dancing, with barbaric frenzy, until it seemed they might in truth scare the devils, or that they, themselves, were possessed of them. The furious energy thrown into the dance held the spectators spellbound. With a flashlight I caught their photographs. As a devil-scarer a flashlight beats dancing, for the whole party immediately decamped.

A Flash Light on the Devil Dancers.

From Kandy it is a steady climb to Nuwara Eliya. The railroad penetrates ravines
and climbs mountain slopes—ever up and up.
This is the region of Ceylon tea—"Lipton's
Best." As we went up the thermometer went
down. When we reached Nuwara Eliya we
were over six thousand feet high,—more
than a mile. It was uncomfortably cool and
rainy, but in the hot season it is a favorite resort for the European residents to escape the
heat of the lowlands. We had parted with
the palms, but we made the acquaintance of
the tree ferns and tea bushes.

At the rear of the town is the highest peak
on the island, over eight thousand feet in ele-
vation. The Cingalese, having plenty of
time, call it Pidaru Talaga, but the Europeans cut it to Pedro. The view from the
summit is well worth the climb. Mountains
and valleys, roughly tumbled, extend away
to Adam's Peak. But our view was short.
A fog from the ocean rolled up the valleys
like a tidal wave, engulfing the lesser mountains and surrounding our peak as with an angry sea.

CHAPTER XXIV.

Calcutta is an English introduction to the real India to be found inland. It is associated with the stirring deeds of the founding of the British Indian Empire. At this capital Lord Clive, Warren Hastings and others, with far-seeing diplomacy and intrepid daring, wove the nets and planned the campaigns that absorbed the native States one after another.

Here was enacted the atrocity of the Black Hole of Calcutta, which led to the overthrow of Bengal, and the founding of the British-Indian Empire. In the early days when Calcutta was a mere trading station of the East India Company, the Nawab of Bengal, having made war on the station, threw one hundred and forty-six of the surrendered garrison into a cell eighteen feet square, ventilated only from a small window high in the wall. It was a sweltering night in July. The Nawab was deaf to the cries of the prisoners dying from suffocation. In

134

Having Their Pictures Taken.

the morning when the doors were opened only twenty-three remained alive.

The news of the atrocity crept along the shore, and went out to sea. It reached Lord Clive, commanding at Madras, and soon his little army, furious for vengeance, overtook the Nawab's superior force on the field of Plassey, annihilated it, and founded the British-Indian Empire.

Since then the Nawab and his descendants have had a good deal of leisure time.

On the site of the prison in which the atrocity was committed now stands the British postoffice. In the yard is preserved a bit of old pavement which, according to a brass tablet nearby, marks the site of the black hole. It is a pity the walls themselves could not have been preserved like the residency buildings at Lucknow, for no monument however grand can touch the heart like the humble ruins where the sons of Britannia fought and died for the little green isle in the northern sea which all English people, the world over, call home.

We rode to the Botanical Garden where the celebrated great banyan tree spreads its branches over many acres. It has over a hundred auxilliary trunks, and is still grow-

ing. On the return drive we visited the new
Jaine temple, and found it a glitter of fragments of colored glass set in stucco, and surrounded by a garden littered with cast iron
Venuses from Europe and porcelain dragons
from Japan, all very new and tawdry.

In Calcutta, according to the custom of
the country, we were introduced to the Indian
bearer or private servant. If one is to continue to exist in India it becomes a dire necessity to employ a bearer who will wait upon
you at the table, attend to your room duties,
prepare your bath, brush and lay out your
clothes, and be a general nuisance so far as
his caste will permit.

This wretched institution of caste is always
in the way. Your bearer's caste may permit
him to bring you clean water, but it will not
permit him to empty the slops. He must employ one of the Sudra caste to do that. The
Sudra caste is the laborer, the tiller of the
soil, creator of wealth; but it is forbidden
that he acquire wealth or learning, or hear
the reading of the sacred books. He and
his children must forever continue despised
Sudras. Caste is the strictest trade union in
the world. If a Hindoo performs the work
or assumes the privileges of another caste he

Snap-Shots by the Wayside.

defiles himself, endangers his soul, and low-
ers the standard of his next incarnation. He
also postpones the time of his final Nirvana—
a dreadful calamity, for next to curry and
rice the Hindoo dearly loves rest.

At night the bearer wraps himself, head
and feet, in a blanket and lies before your
doorway to guard you from robbery by any
unauthorized person. That prerogative he
reserves for himself. This is done, however,
only in the legal and approved system of
commissions.

The poor Bengalese is a yellowish-brown
creature with a striking array of white teeth,
that is, when they are not stained dark red by
chewing the betel nut. His face displays a
fawning smile that seems constantly on the
point of disappearance. He wears a won-
drous turban. A length of cotton cloth
does duty as trousers by being looped
around the thighs with one end brought up
between the legs. Sometimes the other end
is thrown over the shoulder; sometimes a
white cotton jacket is worn. The jacket in-
dictates European culture.

An Indian's prosperity can be judged
by his avoirdupois. Prosperity and
adiposity go together. If the man is

poor his legs are thin, bony shanks with knobs at the knees. The calf is absent, but he is liberally supplied with feet that would leave large marks in the mud, with toes diverging like a chicken's. When he stands, he is inclined to cross his legs like a camp chair. When he sits on his heels he rests his knees comfortably in his armpits. Sometimes by some unaccountable trick of contortion he thrusts his knees entirely out of sight behind his shoulders, and then, viewed from the front, the feet seem to be attached directly to the body like a turtle's. If you see a pair of fat legs projecting from a loin cloth you know whoever lives over the legs is rich, because he is well fed. If he wears shoes, socks and Boston garters you know European culture has attacked his feet and is progressing upwards.

Calcutta is sometimes called "The City of Palaces," owing to the large houses of the English officers. Their houses are necessarily large to accommodate the large number of servants it is customary to care for. This retinue or multitude must make a home seem like an institution.

At sunset we drove on the fashionable boulevard beside the Hoogly river. At that hour it is thronged with equipages of the flower and chivalry of Anglo-Indian, Hindoo and Mohammedan aristocracy. The showy trappings of the horses and the gorgeous liveries of the footmen and outriders form a spectacle that cannot be equalled outside of a circus pageant.

CHAPTER XXV.

In winter the plains of India are terribly hot. Ordinary English is of no use in describing the heat of summer.

We Americans are led to believe that Yuma, Arizona, is the hottest place in the world because it was a resident of Yuma, who having died and gone to Hades, sent back for a blanket. But compared with India in summer, Yuma is said to have a cool and salubrious climate. So the Anglo-Indian goes in summer to Darjeeling on the backbone of the world, to cool off. We went in the winter for the same purpose.

After passing through a tropical plain we reached the Ganges which at this point is a very wide river. During its passage on the steamer we enjoyed an excellent dinner. On the other side we took cars again, and were soon rolled in our blankets on the berths which let down from the sides of the cars.

The next morning we were crossing a brown, dusty, barren plain with frequent groups of mud houses called villages. During the rainy season the plains are green with wheat and barley. The rainy season is expected to come once a year, but sometimes it is careless about it. They have a special God to look after the rain business, too, but he is a lazy, shiftless fellow, as likely to drop the rain into the sea or on the mountains as where it is most needed.

About noon we reached the foothill and changed to mountain cars. These little cars are much like open trolleys. They are built very close to the narrow gauge track and are pulled by a hysterical, little engine that makes a tremendous noise.

We soon plunged into the forest, winding about the hillsides, climbing gullies, and ever turning and curving on a grade so steep that we could feel the cars lift.

At one place we had the novel experience of being run over by our own engine. The train spiraled around a hillock, like a snake chasing its own tail, and then escaped from the top by a bridge to the mountain side. We, in the rear car, saw our own engine crossing the bridge over our heads.

Two men ran ahead scattering sand on the track. They filled their own baskets, too.

There is a story that once one fell asleep on the track while waiting for the train to overtake him and was run over. It was not true, but in other respects it was a good story.

This is the region of jungles and snakes, leopards and tigers. From one of these lonely stations the message was once flashed to the railway headquarters in Calcutta, "Tiger on platform eating station agent; wire instructions." We know this is true because Mark Twain invented it.

We passed many tea plantations where the steep hillside had been terraced. The hill people have decided Mongolian features. They are heavily and dirtily clothed and wear fierce knives thrust in their belts. The women resemble North American Indian women in their way of dressing their hair in long braids, one falling in front of each shoulder, and in their features which are round, flat and copper colored, with high cheek bones. They carry incredible loads on their backs, steadied by bands across the forehead.

We were away above the region of the palms, but the trees of the dense jungle were festooned with orchids. At times we caught glimpses of the plain of Hindustan; and as

Himalaya Children.

we went higher it lengthened and broadened until it was spread out like a map, brown and smoky, and slashed here and there by the silvery ribbons of the streams. Finally a bank of fog came rolling down the valleys, pouring over the cliffs like waterfalls and closing out the view.

When we reached Darjeeling we were over a mile high. For the first time since leaving Japan overcoats were needed. We rode to the hotel in rikishas, along a path that almost overhung a deep valley. I believe it often rains in Darjeeling,—the rest of the time it is foggy. Sometimes Nature runs out of fog, and then the mountains may be seen at their best. The buildings are mortised into the mountains, one end being plunged into the hillside and the other supported on stilts as slender as Hindoo legs.

From the hotel there was a stupendous panorama. Below yawned an abyss of a valley. Away down in its dark depths was a raging torrent. Across the valley was a tree-clad hill. Over its crest, far beyond, arose the rugged tumble of dark mountains whose cliffs and chasms were barred and spotted with fog banks. Still higher, far above the intervening clouds, a snowy peak glittered with the whiteness of everlasting ice. This was Kinchinjanga,—over five miles high. Other peaks, scarcely lower, stretched away into the uncertainty of distance in a gleaming, jagged band of white.

The next morning we arose at four o'clock, and before dawn were stumbling our way on horseback up the trail to Tiger Hill to see the sunrise on Mount Everest, twenty-nine thousand feet high,—the loftiest mountain in the Himalayas.

When we reached the summit, gray dawn was just breaking. We were on a foothill of the first range. In the deep valley between us and the main range the gloom of night still lingered. Beyond this murky chasm rose the abrupt walls of the Himalayas, height on height, cloud-scarred, harsh and forbidding. Peak after peak in snowy confusion led afar and away into the western sky, until peaks and clouds blended in the gray of dawn. Cold, cruel, stupendous, these cloud-defying mountains crush the beholder with their awe-inspiring majesty.

No wonder the Hindoos located their divinities on these inaccessible mountain tops. Brahma, the Creator,—Vishnu, the Preserver,—and Shiva, the Destroyer, hold their courts there in greater seclusion than did Jupiter and Juno on Mount Olympus.

In the east, beyond the purple plains of Hindustan, a crimson line appeared along the horizon. It broadened and lengthened and, flaming upward, crimsoned the edges of the clouds. Here and there cloud upon cloud was touched with gold and copper until the east became a crimson lake, with purple rifts, and golden shores. Then came a brighter glow with the glitter of polished brass, just at the horizon; brighter and brighter it gleamed, and a ray of sunlight shot straight to the snowy peaks, suffusing their snow-fields with a rosy radiance.

In the native bazaars may be seen a few Thibetans and many strange people of the hill tribes. The women are heavily loaded with ornaments of silver and brass curiously set with turquois, malachite and agate. In these bazaars may be bought many strange and curious things, such as prayer wheels, idols, and charms made of human ashes from Thibet. These charms are carried in small boxes suspended from a cord around the neck. The boxes are sometimes of brass, and sometimes of tin taken from Standard Oil cans,—which shows how the light of American civilization is penetrating the remotest regions of Asia.

These hill people are good salesmen. When the traveler appears in the street the glad tidings spread rapidly. From doorways and booths come the traders with obsequious smiles, each with a curio of more or less antiquity half concealed in his voluminous sleeve. As each one offers his wares he explains in broken English:

"This Buddha brought from a monastery in Napaul."

"This prayer-wheel was used by the Grand Llama of Thibet and smuggled over the border."

"This bracelet, very antique, was worn by the Squegee of Gazoozulum."

Another serious old trader produced the short brass knife used by Buddhist priests as a symbol of office, and solemnly related this strange history:

"Sacred knife not made by man,—no," and he rolled his eyes devoutly, "made by hand of God himself and dropped from heaven in a thunder-cloud to mountain top, where Grand Llama found it buried deep in rock. Grand Llama with it slew seven dragons of the air and then present to me, because I hon-

est man,—not lie; but I, very poor man.   I
sell you for sixteen rupees."

The Philosopher said I would be sold
if I bought it; and as the story seemed
the most remarkable thing about it, I kept the
story and returned the knife.   The "honest
man" would then take ten rupees, and finally
would take an offer.

There was a brass God from Thibet.   At
least by calling on the reserve stock of
credulity wise travelers should keep on hand
for emergencies,—I was willing to believe it
came from Thibet.   This brass idol from
Thibet had a beautiful carbuncle (the jewel
kind) on his neck.   I longed to possess
it and bargained for it according to custom,
but did not buy it, because the owner would
not come down the usual fifty per cent.
When I was seated in the rikisha, he sadly
shook his head and repeated, "God very antique."   I expected he would relent, but the
last I saw of him he was standing irresolute
in his doorway with the idol in his hand.
And so it passed out of my life forever, and
I have mourned it ever since—that brass
God from Thibet with the carbuncle on its
neck.

The ride down the mountain was a coast, a

toboggan slide, a shute the shutes, and a
merry-go-round all in one.   When dusk came
on, a torch was lighted above the engine.
That was thoughtful.   It lighted up the forest, gave the only light for the cars, and kept
the tigers off.

The next morning at dawn we had breakfast on the boat crossing the Ganges.   The
waters were glassy.   The reflections of the
trees on the low banks were perfect.   Here
and there widening circles of ripples showed
where fish came to the surface to get the early
flies.

When we reached the opposite bank hundreds of natives were performing their devotions and ablutions in the sacred stream,
or sitting silently on their heels, their limbs
benumbed by the chill.   They were apparently engaged in sluggish contemplation.
The sun came up a dull red globe, the Ganges
responded, the mists of morning lifted and
the natives one by one arose and went their
way.

CHAPTER XXVI.

BENARES, THE SACRED CITY.

Benares is celebrated in India as the most sacred of cities,—and elsewhere as the place where the chiseled brass comes from.

Here we had the first glimpse of the real India of our dreams. Here are the remains of the oriental magnificence and wealth of Ormuz and of Ind. Here we saw the real Indian almost free from the influences that are leading him gradually— very, very gradually,—out of the darkness of superstition into the light of the new civilization. Here he is unpuffed up by the yeast of British culture. Here pilgrims come from the uttermost regions of India to worship the savage-looking idols, or rather worship before them, and to bathe in the sacred waters of the Ganges.

As Mecca is sacred to the Mohammedan, so is Benares sacred to the Hindoo. A pilgrimage to these places is a virtuous and soul-benefiting thing, and greatly improves the chances of a happy hereafter.

The first place visited was the Monkey

Temple, dedicated to the Monkey God.
Here innumerable monkeys make their home
and a very good living, for it is the custom
for visitors to buy nuts from the gate-keeper.
The monkeys collect the nuts as you go in.
They are very entertaining while the rations
last, and then, like some human guests, they
make off for newer friends, or scamper up
the roof and deliberately turn their backs, cutting your acquaintance.

In this temple we saw the ceremony of hair-
cutting on a five-year-old girl. The child entered the court-yard in the company of parents and relatives, followed apparently by
friends and neighbors. In the rear of the
procession came musicians with flutes, cymbals and drums, and several nautch girls singing a monotonous air with considerable violence. All the musicians and nautch girls
seated themselves in a circle on the pavement
of the open court with the maiden in the
center.

The priest in ceremonial robes proceeded
to shear her locks and shave her scalp. In
the meantime the musicians beat the tom-
toms, crashed the cymbals and brought forth
ear-piercing shrieks from the flutes, while the
nautch girls sang a weird chant. The mon-

keys, perched upon the cornices, gravely
watched the proceedings. The child being
shorn and shaven, her garments were removed and others of gorgeous silk, resplendent with tinsel and spangles, were placed
upon her, and garlands of flowers were placed
about her neck. Then the nautch girls ceased
their singing and danced a squirmy dance,
waving their bare arms to lively music.

The guide explained that this was a religious rite preliminary to a betrothal, which
left its real nature in considerable doubt. It
was evidently one of the numerous religious
shaves practiced upon the Hindoos. Many
of the ordinary things of life are considered
as religious rites, at which a priest must
officiate, with his usual fee. Between fees to
the priests, and taxes to the government, the
thin-legged Hindoo has a narrow margin for
curry and rice.

Close to the Monkey Temple is the house
and garden of the Holy Man of Benares.
This man is a real God, and was, long before
he died, for the good man has been dead and
in Nirvana some time. He was a very
learned Yogi, and in such a state of perfect
sanctification that nothing whatever interested him. The guide pointed out his flower-

strewn grave under a marble canopy and explained that the accepted way for a good Hindoo to return to dust is by burning; but if one prefers to be buried it is allowable, provided he is buried alive, for no dead body should contaminate the earth. Therefore, the sacred man being full of years, and near unto death, and knowing through his occult power the exact moment when death would overtake him, caused himself to be buried alive just one hour before he died.

To the Philosopher's materialistic mind it was a little puzzling to understand how it was that he could be killed by burying just one hour before he died a natural death. The guide entered into a long explanation about the astral body and other things theosophical, trying to make the point clear to the Philosopher, but all that he seemed to grasp was that the man was dead, and that it cost something to see where he was buried.

The Temple of the Sacred Bulls is a place that fortunately can be viewed by unbelievers from a platform. The Philosopher desired to get a nearer photograph of the sacred beasts in their sanctuary, but the floor of the temple, being a stable, was as dirty as neglect and wet weather could make it. After long hesitation he resigned himself to the probably ruin of his shoes for the sake of the photograph, and proceeded to cautiously step down into the court; but an argus-eyed attendant saw his design and in great alarm stopped him, saying that the feet of an unbeliever would pollute the place. The Philosopher desisted, but his feelings were hurt.

These sacred cattle roam at will about the city, helping themselves to the best in the way of food from the merchant's supplies. When they blockade the narrow streets the people give them resounding thumps in spite of their sanctity, but they move out of the way with the deliberation and dignity becoming their lofty estate. The ancient wise men knew that by making them sacred they would preserve through any misfortune the species of this most useful beast of burden.

The Golden Temple is a small affair but very sacred. It is overlaid, inside and out, with yellow gold. We were not permitted to enter.

Far more curious was the less pretentious temple dedicated to the Elephant God. In the center of the temple, on an altar, was a stone post called the lingam. Offerings of flowers were at its base. The Hindoo my-

thology ascribes sex to the creators of heaven
and earth. The lingam represents the male
element. The female element is indicated by
two interlaced equal-sided triangles forming
a six-pointed star like a masonic emblem. Before these altars the natives worship, gar-
landing the lingam with flowers, and pouring
upon it water from brass urns which they have
brought on their heads from the Ganges.

The most interesting part of Benares, and
perhaps of all India, is the river front. Here
is congregated all that is Indian in custom,
architecture and religion. It is a very sacred
spot, for here one of their divinities, the Elephant God, made his last appearance upon
earth, and a river direct from Paradise finds
its underground union with the Ganges.

Benares is the most ancient city of India,
and is expected to last until it becomes a part
of Paradise itself. The city is so sacred that
any person who dies within its limits will go
straight to heaven regardless of his religion
or the lack of it. It is a very popular place
to die in. But the other side of the river opposite the city is profane and accursed, and
whoever dies there will be born again a jackass.

So firmly grounded is this belief that while

The River Front at Benares.

the sacred side is crowded with palaces and temples and thronged with humanity, the opposite side of the river, a few hundred feet away, is abandoned by man. One can see the jackals, wild dogs and other wild beasts roaming the barren sands in perfect security.

The Philosopher had a new scheme. He proposed to lay out a first addition to Benares on the jackass side of the river and boom it in true western fashion with brass bands, barbecues and auctions, and give a non-jackass insurance policy with every corner lot.

Ridiculous! Who ever heard of a non-jackass insurance policy?

The Rajah of Benares has a palace on the other side of the river, but some distance up. He is, however, so suspicious of the location that whenever any of his household are taken ill they are hustled across the river to the guaranteed safe side to await there the result of their disease. If they survive they rejoice that they have escaped the superlative joys of heaven, and give thanks for the cure to the prayers of the priest, but if they succumb, the result is ascribed to the mysterious dispensation of an all-wise and unscrupulous providence.

We took an observation boat and floated

down the river past scenes so strange, so bizarre, that they baffle description. The river makes a majestic curve with Benares on the convexity. This is called Sheva's Bow. The level of the city is perhaps a hundred feet above the level of the river. The bluff is occupied by a continuous row of temples and palaces belonging to the various princes and rulers of the Indias; for this is the Newport, the Long Branch, and the Ocean Grove of the Hindoo world amalgamated into one bewildering mass.

At certain seasons of the year all good Hindoos, brahmin, prince or peasant, make a pilgrimage to Benares to worship and bathe in the Ganges, and to carry to their homes some of the sacred water.

From the palaces and temples on the bluff, stone steps and terraces descend to the water's edge. These steps, or gauts as they are called, swarm with the multitude, robed in white and many colors.

Standing waist deep in the water were men, women and children seriously performing their devotions. As the Hindoo walks down the steps into the river he clasps his hands, bows to the Goddess Gunga, dips his hands in the water and applies it to his forehead, breast, and mouth, as certain prayers are repeated. At times the hands are clasped, or elevated, or the body bent in adoration. The devotions being completed, a brass urn is filled with the water, and he returns to the steps where he proceeds to wash his clothes. His winding sheet is removed, washed by whipping on the stones and trailing in the water, then dried in the wind. The winding cloth is then replaced around the body and the loin cloth surreptitiously removed and subjected to the same process. When in this manner his body, his soul and his raiment are cleansed, and he is ready to re-enter the streets, he approaches a priest who sits under a wide-spreading basket-work umbrella calling out incantations. He kneels before the priest and receives upon his forehead the mark in paint that signifies his caste and announces to all the world that he has fulfilled his religious duties. He then departs up the steps carrying his brass urn of sacred water upon his head.

We passed box-like pedestals standing on the terraces. These were the suttee towers where formerly widows burned themselves on the funeral pyres of their husbands. By the river bank were the earthly remains of a few Hindoos, the men wrapped head and body in white, and the women in red winding sheets. Some were lying with their feet in the sacred stream, while others who had received the last rites of the river were being consumed on the funeral pyres.

A Rajah was ascending the steps to pay his respects to a Holy Man. A gorgeous red cloak with gold spangles hung from his shoulders. An attendant held an umbrella-like affair over his head, and four guards marched behind. At the steps was moored the Rajah's boat, a two-storied affair, the upper deck shaded with awnings, under which a silver chair stood on rich rugs and tiger skins.

Along the river bank could be seen those religious fanatics called fakirs or yogis. Some sat in profound meditation, their naked bodies and bowed heads covered with ashes. One, in whose dark eyes burned the fire of mania, darted about the throng in aimless activity. He was naked except for the most rudimentary loin cloth. His body was marked in stripes with ashes, like a zebra, and his hair hung in matted ropes to the ground.

One fakir has achieved earthly fame and spiritual credit as the standing man. He stood upon the left leg, the right foot resting

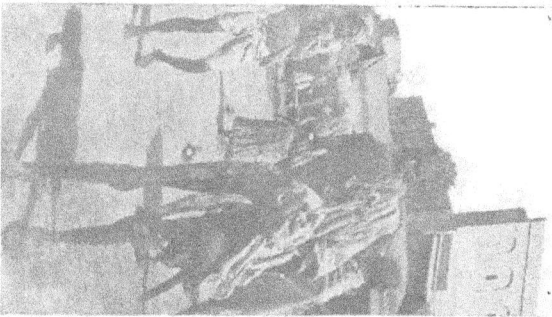

Indian Fakeers—Sacred and Dirty.

on the left knee. Both arms were extended
straight up and clasped over his head. He
stood upon a post in the water balanced like
a stork. It was said that every day for years
he had been in that position and no one had
seen him move during business hours. Others
attain a state of ecstacy and remain in a fixed
position until muscular atrophy results. It
is a form of voluntary catalepsy possible only
to those religious monomaniacs who have arrived at that beatific state by continuous auto-
hypnotism. Some of the things they are said
to do are apparently impossible, such as sitting or lying on beds of sharp tacks, or walk-
ing in the fire without injury. These persons
are revered as saints by the Hindoos.

One of these saints sat alone on a post in
the water. He wore a coarse brown cloak,
and a little brown rag fluttered in the wind
from a stick planted beside him. He was
greatly respected. He was a continuous-pray-
ing yogi. He prayed aloud, and whenever
he bowed to the river he held his nose. This
was not strange, inasmuch as the river at that
point had more the appearance of mullaga-
tawny soup than a sacred stream, carrying as
it did the city sewage and sundry vegetable
and animal remains, for which the citizens

had no further use. However, these details did not disturb the pilgrims, who strong in their faith and belief, considered nothing impure or unclean which had come in contact with the sacred waters.

But, as I said before, this particular saint was holding his nose. As it is customary for travelers to ask questions of a guide whether he could possibly know the answer or not, we inquired the reason for the aforesaid noseholding, and immediately struck a well of curious information.

It appears that the Hindoo worship is very elaborate in its formality, and their Gods very particular about due respect being shown them, each requiring a special formality. As there are thirty-three millions of Gods, three million of whom have terrible reputations for revenge if slighted, it will be clear that it is not all jam keeping them good-natured.

The guide said that when a Hindoo in the course of his prayers utters the word Brahma he must press the right nostril with the right thumb. When Sheva is implored the right forefinger must compress the left nostril. Vishnu claims another finger, and other Gods have reserved the remaining digits. When their names are uttered aloud, and in rapid succession, the effect is somewhat startling to the ear and shocking to the sight.

The guide could not tell the Philosopher what Gods were appealed to when the thumb was applied to the tip of the nose, and the fingers gently undulated, but after some deliberation concluded that it might be an appeal to the Christian Gods as he had seen the rite performed among the English soldiers.

This guide confidently assured us that he was a very truthful man, good Hindoo, very high caste, Brahma pundit caste, privileged to cook food for the high priests, and was above accepting presents for charity; but if we were pleased with his services he would not refuse a present in case such great lords as we should offer it, and he would thank us kindly, and appreciate it very much as he was a very poor man and he hoped we would not forget him. At that point the Philosopher remarked that would be about all the biography we cared to know, and he might thereafter, as in the past, confine his remarks to history and fiction.

The Mohammedan mosque whose two slender minarets are the most prominent landmarks in Benares, was built by the last Grand Mogul, a Mohammedan Emperor, who de-

stroyed a temple of Sheva to make room for
it. The Hindoos believe it was this act of
sacrilege which brought ruin upon him and
his house. Along the river front are several
half buried and ancient palaces destroyed by
an earthquake. Our guide explained that
foundations are insecure because the river
from Paradise flows beneath, and if the gods
were displeased they would now and then let
a palace drop in.

Ceremonial Bathing in the Sacred Ganges.

CHAPTER XXVII.

LUCKNOW AND CAWNPORE—THE INDIAN MUTINY.

From Benares we crossed a monotonous plain of wheat fields nearing the harvest. When the grain crop is good there is plenty in India, but when the rains fail, as they frequently do, the poor coolie starves. Some important irrigation works undertaken by the government are expected to relieve the suffering, but India is generally hungry. Under the old regime the population was kept down somewhat by wars, thuggee, suttee and drowning of female infants, all of which have been put down by the English who prefer to dig canals for irrigating and let the population grow.

It is a dusty, hot ride to Lucknow, enlivened by an occasional glimpse of an elephant laboring in the fields or playing omnibus for a family, groups of wild monkeys swinging from the trees, or herons stalking pompously through the ponds.

In Lucknow we were reminded not only of the splendor of the Kings of Oude, which can be touched lightly as a thing apart, but of Anglo-Saxon suffering and heroism in connection with the Indian mutiny of 1857, which must bring to every English-speaking person a thrill of sympathy and pride.

The defence of the English Residency against overwhelming odds, and the valor of the rescuing columns who cut their bloody way through hordes of rebels, are as heroic as any deeds since history began.

The causes of the rebellion of the native troops were many. Perhaps one of the most important was insufficient regard given by the English officials for the rules of caste and religious prejudices which, to the Indians are more important than life itself. For instance the cartridges were coated with the fat of cows and sheep. To handle such animal products and especially to hold them in the mouth as the rules required was to be defiled. It took a mutiny to change that rule.

The consideration given the religious sensibilities of the natives at that time is indicated by Bayard Taylor who visited India shortly before the mutiny and wrote:

"In India all places of worship, except the inner shrines—the Holy of Holies—are open to the conquerors, who walk in, booted and spurred, where the Hindoo or Moslem put their shoes off their feet. I should willingly have complied with this form as I did in other Moslem countries, but was told that it was now never expected of a European and would be, in fact, a depreciation of his dignity."

The English Resident Agent occupied a mansion surrounded by the barracks of the native troops or sepoys in the service of the East India Company. At Lucknow less than seven hundred remained faithful. They, with about seven hundred English troops, intrenched themselves in the Residency grounds and gathered therein all the foreign residents and native sympathizers, men, women and children, to the number of twenty-nine hundred souls. In this frail encampment they were besieged for nearly six months by fifty thousand fanatical rebels with artillery. The grounds were raked with musket bullets and the buildings riddled with cannon shots. The men lived day and night in the trenches, and the women and children in cellars and underground passage-ways.

After three months the thunder of the guns of Sir Henry Havelock's relieving army was heard on the Cawnpore road. Foot by foot they fought their way to the Residency, but arrived so weakened and decimated that they could only join the besieged garrison and await further relief.

At last it came with Sir Colin Campbell's Highlanders. By forced marches in the heat of the Indian summer, during which the temperature ranged betwen 120 and 138 degrees in the shade, it cut its bloody tunnel through hordes of rebels by continuous fighting against tremendous odds. Nothing deterred them. After viewing the slaughter of the women and children at Cawnpore, their fury knew no bounds. It was a continuous massacre. At last the Residency was relieved, but of the gallant band of twenty-nine hundred only nine hundred were alive.

The Residency buildings remain as they were left by the siege,—crumbled, blackened, shot-riddled ruins,—gradually being overgrown with ivy—fitting monuments to English valor.

At Lucknow we got our first impressions of the glory of the Mongul Emperors and of the splendid palaces they built. The last Nawab, when reduced to semi-imbecility by dissipation, spent his time dancing the nautch, while the English annexed his kingdom, thereby adding another cause for the mutiny.

The Imambarra, the tomb of a Nawab, is
a dazzling white marble building capped with
groups of white pavilions. In its gardens are
fountains, and some British lions painted
with stripes to represent tigers. The Indians
do not understand lions, but have a whole-
some fear of tigers.

The massive and ornate Turkish gate,
nearby, stands out, a shining white pile
against the wonderful blue of the sky. In
these interior cities the soot and smoke of
burning coal are unknown and the buildings
retain their pure, white beauty untarnished
for hundreds of years.

We stopped for an afternoon at Cawnpore on our way to Agra. There is nothing
to see at Cawnpore except the monuments to
the garrison massacred during the mutiny.
Here the garrison after a hopeless defense
capitulated to the rebels, only to be murdered
at leisure. Most of the women and children
were kept prisoners until the rebel leader,
Nana Sahib, realized that the English would
retake the place. When the roar of their
cannon drew near he ordered the prisoners
slaughtered. Three Mohammedan and two
Hindoo soldiers were selected for the bloody
work. With naked swords they entered the

inclosure where the defenseless women and children were encaged. When the scream of the last terrified woman was silenced; the sob of the last infant was stilled, they were thrown, the dead and dying, into a well, and when a few hours later the rescuing army came raging in, alas, there were none alive to rescue.

About that court is now an octagonal Gothic screen of the purest white marble, and over the well stands a marble cross, and an angel with hands crossed meekly upon the breast.

It was midnight when our train rolled across the iron bridge that spans the Jumna at Agra. In the moonlight we could see the swelling domes of the Jumna Musjid mosque marked with lines of red sandstone and white marble; and the frowning battlements of the great fort at Akbar, the greatest of the Mongul Emperors,—soldier, philosopher and law-giver. Within this grim fortification are palaces of such richness and beauty that only in the tales of the Arabian Nights can their equal be found.

CHAPTER XXVIII.

AGRA AND THE FORT OF AKBAR.

In Agra, as in the other interior towns of India, the foreign hotels are located in the cantonment, or district devoted to the barracks of the British troops, the residences of the officers, missionaries and foreign merchants outside of the native city. These quarters are very pleasant places in which to live. The semi-European houses are embowered in ample gardens bordering the broad streets.

The hotels in central India are much alike. They have one story wings with porticos upon which open the doors of the sleeping apartments. These apartments are whitewashed stone rooms, each with a window high up near the ceiling for ventilation, and a small one by the door to look through. There is a narrow, hard bed with a Turkey red punkah swinging above it. The floors are stone or cement and a small rug tries to make it look cheerful.

In the rear is a dressing room and bath. The three-foot stone wall built nearly around one corner is not a fortification against another mutiny, but the bath compartment, and on its cold stone floor rests a three-shilling tin foot-bath—the storied tub of the Englishman.   Forty dollars worth of stone fence around forty cents worth of plumbing.   It was aggravating.   The Philosopher said:

"While we are in Agra we should expect to be aggravated."

A pun is a protozoic form of wit, and an incitant to crime.

All through the chilly night the bearer sleeps on the portico in front of your bedroom door.   In the early dawn he crawls out of his cocoon of blankets in which he has wrapped himself, clangs the tin tub on the stone floor, fills it with tepid water; brings chota hazrid, (early breakfast of tea and toast,) then sits upon his heels awaiting orders.   About ten o'clock breakfast is served in the dining room.   It is a substantial meal— if you get it—a contingency depending upon the agility and diplomacy of your bearer and upon the caprice of a not over scrupulous providence.   That function being completed, the traveler delivers himself into the hands of the guide to be shown things.

I had a theory that we should begin with

the less important sights and work up by
easy stages saving the Taj Mahal for the
last, as a grand climax; but the Philosopher
had in mind the old story of the Irishman who
being invited to eat all he could at a
restaurant, began at the top and ordered
something in French. It proved to be soup,
he ordered the next—that also was soup; he
tried again and drew soup, and thus proceeded until he had taken each kind of soup and
was ready to burst. When he saw the really
good things coming on for others, he remarked, as he sadly withdrew, " 'Tis the chance of
me life, and me full of soup." Therefore, the
Philosopher, for fear of being over-fed on
lesser sights, went off alone to see the Taj
Mahal, while I went to the fort.

Akbar, the Wise and Great, founded
Agra and built therein a fort seventy feet
high and nearly two miles around. In it he
and his successors Shah Jehan, Aurenzebe and
others built palaces as beautiful as dreams.

As we entered the fort our carriage crossed
an empty moat, passed under heavy arch-
ways, through murky tunnels, and finally
stopped before the Judgment Hall of Akbar,
the Solomon of the East, the greatest of the
Grand Monguls. This hall is a loggia open

on three sides. Colonnades of marble pillars
support the groined marble ceiling. In the
closed side is an elevated niche ornamented
with mosaics of birds and flowers. This is
the Judgment seat of Akbar. His conquests
were of short duration. The Empire which
he founded has crumbled to pieces; his palaces
are now show places for tourists, but his laws,
—the Code Akbar,—are still used in parts
of India. The good men do lives after them,
and the evil dies with them,—perhaps.

We passed through a few rooms of the red
sandstone palace of Aurenzebe and saw stone
ceilings and walls engraved all over in the
most dainty designs of arabesque and flowers,
remaining as sharp and clear as when the
sculptors completed their work three hundred
years ago. In some rooms the painting and
gilding on the sculptured walls are still bright
and beautiful.

The palace of Shah Jehan is of dazzling
white marble cresting the red sandstone walls
of the fort. There are majestic halls, airy
pavilions, and sunken arenas where tigers
and elephants fought for the amusement of
the court; and the Persian gardens where the
sprites of the harem played hide and seek
among the rose and jessamine bowers. On

The Vacant Throne of the Moguls.

three sides of this garden were their apartments.

On a marble terrace overlooking the garden stands the black marble platform upon which the Great Mogul, the King of Kings, sat cross-legged on his jeweled throne, under a canopy of silken tapestry.

The black marble platform is now barren; on its beautiful polished surface is a red stain, and through its ponderous body is a fissure. This is evidence of a miraculous manifestation, for legend has it that the platform rent itself in twain and wept blood, when the Maharretta conqueror ascended it, and again when an English Viceroy seated himself thereon.

The Golden Pavilion, the Jewel Tower and the Jessamine Pavilion are tiny retreats, bird cages in inlaid marble, for the beauties of the harem. In the mosaic floors are sculptured basins for fountains of rose water, behind which colored lights were placed.

There is the Persian pavilion whose roof is a single block of marble sculptured with a design of Persian roses. From the capitals of the supporting pillars droop marble rosebuds so delicately beautiful that the soul of the beholder sings with delight. In this pavilion sat the beauties of the harem with silver rods and silken line, angling for gold fish in the fountain below.

In the harem are the wonderful apartments of the mirrored bath. These rooms are as still and cool as marble caves. They were lighted only by many tiny lamps set in niches behind colored glasses. From the walls gushed fountains sparkling with the colors of concealed lights and falling in glittering cascades into marble pools to flow away, babbling from room to room over a mosaic bed.

In such an enchanted grotto, with its silken carpets, its mellow lights, its splashing fountains, its heavy perfumes, and its myriad reflections of the merry nymphs of the harem— the King was wont to take his recreation.

In one of the rooms of the palace upon the ceiling is inscribed in Persian poetry:

"If there is a paradise on earth,—it is here,—it is here,—it is here."

CHAPTER XXIX.

THE TAJ MAHAL.

The drive from the hotel to the Taj was
through broad streets bordered by trees. On
approaching the entrance there appeared on
either side massive ruins of caravansaries and
palaces; and then came into view, an imposing building in red sandstone capped with
numerous white marble pavilions. The
building is pierced with an immense pointed
archway, and is ornamented with bands, designs and texts from the Koran in white marble. Noble as this building is, it is only the
gateway to the garden of the Taj. I left
the carriage and entered, and beheld in the
distance a gleaming white bubble of a dome
resting so lightly on a sculptured pile of marble that it seemed to float in the air rather
than press upon its foundation. Leading up
to the Taj, through a grove of laurel and
lemon trees, is an avenue of Italian cypresses.
There is a mosaic pavement in this avenue
and through its center is a row of fountains
playing in a lily pool.

The Taj stands on a marble platform as a

jewel casket stands on a table, its eight sides carved and inlaid in black marble with Arabic texts from the Koran. Dominating the four smaller domes is the grand central dome, two-thirds of a globe, with the top sharpened to a point. At the corners of the masonry platform, but apart from the Taj itself, stand four marble minarets, like giant candles before a shrine.

The Taj impresses with the magnitude of its mass, the airy grace of its style,. and the detail of its carved and inlaid marbles. It is love at first sight for there is in the picture a charm which mere words cannot express. It is proportion, and proportion is art, and words are powerless before art.

I sat on a bench in the garden and contemplated its beauties, and they grew more entrancing as the hours passed. The Taj is like a lover who at one moment commands with his over-powering personality and at another cajoles with a caress. At one moment it seemed like a mountain of ice, at another an intangible cloud, at another an onyx casket inlaid with ebony.

When Noor Jehan died following the fortunes of war, with Shah Jehan in far Cashmere, he vowed he would build for her a

tomb whose beauty could never be surpassed.
For seventeen years, thousands toiled. At
last when deposed and old and full of sor-
row, Shah Jehan was near unto death in a
narrow cell, where for seven years he had
been a prisoner in his own palace, he begged
the son who had deposed and imprisoned him,
that he might see again before he died, the
tomb of his Noor Jehan. He was carried to the
jessamine pavilion under whose jeweled marble arches he had known with her what joy
it was to live; and breathed his last with his
eyes resting on the marble domes that gleamed beyond the sandy bed of the Jumna.
There his love awaited him, and there he
rests by her side.

I visited the Taj again in the evening, and
sitting alone by the reflecting waters of the
fountains, contemplated its beauty, gleaming
white and pure in the magic of the pale
moonlight. Then it seemed a pearl palace
from the paradise of dreams; a fitting casket
for Noor Jehan, the pearl of the palace, "The
Light of the Harem," of Moore's immortal
poem.

On entering the Taj one marvels at the
detail of the ornamentation. The light comes
faintly through screens of marble filigree.

The sarcophagi of Shah Jehan and his Queen are in the center, inscribed with the ninety-nine names of God and extracts from the Koran. They are also inlaid with semi-precious stones, such as agate, carnelian, malachite, bloodstone, and coral in floral garlands. The lace-like marble screens that encircle the sarcophagi, and the walls themselves are inlaid in Persian designs with the same beautiful stones. The wainscoting of marble slabs of ivory purity are carved in relief with conventional designs of the lily, iris, tulip and primrose.

There is holy calm and hush in the Taj. The mind is overwhelmed with its beauty and dignity. There is nothing gaudy; nothing inharmonious. With all its richness it conveys an impression of purity and simplicity. It breathes of noble thoughts and a mighty love. Shah Jehan may rest content. The tomb of his well-beloved is not surpassed.

The Taj Mahal.

CHAPTER XXX.

FUTTEHPORE-SIKREE, THE DESERTED CITY.

We drove to the deserted city Futtehpore-Sikree, built by Akbar. On a hill overlooking the fertile plains for miles and miles, stands a walled city with red sandstone palaces, and marble mosques with carving as beautiful as lace, and as perfect as when deserted, over three hundred years ago. No conquering army has destroyed an arch. No vandal hand has marred a pillar. The rooms lack only furniture, rugs and draperies to make them again suitable for the throngs and pomp of a potentate.

Kipling gives a perfect picture of the deserted city in these words:

"What do you think of a big, red, dead city built of red sandstone, with raw, green aloes growing between the stones, lying out neglected on honey-colored sands? There are forty dead kings there, each in a gorgeous tomb finer than all the others. You look at the palaces and streets and shops and tanks, and think that men must live there, till you find a wee, gray squirrel rubbing its nose all

alone in the market-place, and a jeweled peacock struts out of a carved doorway and
spreads its tail against a marble screen as fine-
pierced as point lace. Then a monkey—a
little black monkey—walks through the main
square to get a drink from a tank forty feet
deep. He slides down the creepers to the
water's edge, and a friend holds him by the
tail in case he should fall in. When evening
comes and the lights change, it is as though
you stood in the heart of a king-opal. A little before sundown, as punctually as clock-
work, a big, bristly wild boar, with all his
family following, trots through the city gate,
churning the foam at his tusks. You climb
on the shoulder of a blind, black, stone god
and watch that pig choose himself a palace for
the night and stump in wagging his tail.
Then the night-wind gets up, and the sands
move, and you hear the desert outside the
city singing: 'Now I lay me down to sleep,'
and everything is dark till the moon rises."

The palace of Miriam, Akbar's Portuguese Christian wife, has been refurnished as
an official residence, and affords an example
of how cozy and homelike these old palaces
were. Akbar was, like Solomon, a very liberal man in religious matters. Himself a

Mohammedan, he took a wife from each of the religions of his dominions that through her each denomination might have a sure and and private means of reaching his ear.

In the palace of Miriam is a fresco of the Annunciation. In the palace of another wife are frescoes of the Hindoo God, Ganeish; and in the others are illustrations of Persian poems.

We noticed the frequent repetition in the stone carvings of the six-pointed star, or double triangle, similar to the emblem of masonry. But here it is used in its religious significance symbolizing the female element of the world's creation, as the lingam symbolizes the male element in the creation of all things animate and inanimate. This is one of the most ancient symbols in Brahminism, and was doubtless ancient in the time of Solomon.

Whether the Jews brought masonry from their captivity in Babylon; and if so, whether the Babylonians in turn derived it from the primitive religion of India, are questions which our Masonic friends may be able to answer.

We also noticed carvings of the Greek cross. It is recorded that Akbar once replied to the Jesuits who approached him: "What would you have? Behold! I have more crosses now on my palaces than you have on your churches."

Many of us thought the Congress of Religions held at the Columbian Exhibition was the first of its kind; but the wise Akbar held one in Futtehpore-Sikree over three hundred years ago. On the main gateway to the mosque, the most imposing building on this hill of palaces, is carved in stone the following:

"Jesus, on whom be peace, said: 'The world is a bridge, pass over it, but build no house there. He who hopeth for an hour may hope for eternity. The world lasts but for an hour; spend it in devotion; the rest is unseen.' "

This is singularly like, "Lay not up for yourselves treasures upon earth where moth and rust doth corrupt and where thieves break through and steal."

An intelligent and highly educated Mohammedan explained this surprising recognition of Jesus in the following words:

'Mohammedans recognized Jesus as one of the great Prophets, only below Mohammed and Moses in importance. Moses was

greater because he gave the ten command-
ments, one of which is continually broken by
the Christians when they make graven images
of Christ, Mary, or the saints, and bow down
before them. We Mohammedans follow
that law, and use no pictures or images in
our worship. We consider Mohammed a
greater Prophet than Jesus because he came
later and superseded him. Neither Jesus nor
Mohammed was a God, but only prophets.
Our cry is "God is God, and Mohammed is
His Prophet." If you should tell a Mohammedan that God could be killed by man, or
that God died, and was dead for three days,
he would say it is impossible. God is immortal and therefore cannot die."

CHAPTER XXXI.

DELHI, THE DELIGHTFUL.

Delhi is said to be the oldest capital in the world. It was the capital of an empire when Jerusalem was a barren rock. Within the area of ten miles square there are the remains of seven cities in various stages of ruin. How many have entirely disappeared no one knows. We entered the present city through the Cashmere Gate which was battered and scarred by English cannon during the mutiny when the city was retaken by storm.

The old fort of Shah Jehan is not as interesting as that of Akbar at Agra, because much of it has been destroyed. The gateway is gay with the capping pavilions in the light and airy style of the Moguls, and it is somewhat of a shock to encounter, the first thing on passing through this gateway, the modern barracks of Tommy Atkins constructed in the cheapest and most unornamental manner.

The Audience Hall of Shah Jehan has been whitewashed, thus making light of its dignity. Further on we passed through rooms where

184

the whitewash blunderer had committed desecrations equivalent to a crime. Entire ceilings in marble, exquisitely carved, then painted and gilded with masterly art, have been ruined by the whitewash brush. The English have attempted to repair the damage by a restoration, but the expense was so ruinous that it was abandoned. When one sees entire ceilings and walls where precious paintings in marvelous colors can still be faintly traced through the coat of whitewash, one wonders what manner of man could have ordered such wanton destruction. Much of the palace has been destroyed to make room for barracks, but there still remains the throne room, the most beautiful hall in the world.

From the marble floor rises a forest of marble pillars whose arches, inlaid and embroidered with semi-precious stones, support a ceiling with myriads of pendants painted in green, azure and gold. The screens of marble filigree and the marble walls are inlaid with colored stones in garlands of flowers,—the leaves of malachite and the roses of coral or carnelian in the same manner as in the Taj Mahal. In this hall stood the peacock throne, a blaze of diamonds, sapphires, emeralds, rubies and pearls. The

throne was carried to Persia by the conqueror
Nadir Shah.   Only the marble pedestal remains.   Once there was a massive silver ceiling, but the Mahratta conquerors melted it
down for loot.   When the beauty of the hall
is still so great in spite of the pillage of
many conquerors, what must it have been
when Shah Jehan, in a cloak of scintillating
diamonds, sat upon the peacock throne, surrounded by the splendors of the Mogul court?

A ride through the ancient ruined cities
about Delhi is full of the interest that attaches
to the tumbling tombs of tyrants, and of
mighty monarchs whose names are forgotten.
There are ruins of observatories with astronomical and mathematical instruments
and contrivances where, perhaps, the wise
men of Chaladee studied astronomy and as-
trology.   Here Jey Sing, the royal astronomer who succeeded the Rajahs of Amber and
founded Jaipur, reformed the calendar about
1693.   His astronomical observations were
wonderfully accurate.   The gnomons, dials,
quadrants, and so forth, are on a gigantic
scale, built of solid masonry.   There are
also many curious instruments whose purpose
cannot be guessed.   The "Wise Men of the
East" were very real men.

Eleven miles away is the Kutub Minar, a mighty tower, two hundred and forty feet high, fluted and banded with carving. Its origin is enveloped in mystery. In the courtyard of an ancient temple nearby is a wrought iron pillar older than Christianity. An inscription in Sanskrit announces that it is: "The arm of fame of Rajah Dhava, who conquered his neighbors and won the undisputed sovereignty of the earth." Who was Rajah Dhava? This is the only evidence that he ever existed.

CHAPTER XXXII.

A NAUTCH DANCE.

I have seen a nautch dance. In my boyhood I read the tales of travelers, and their descriptions conjured up in my imagination pictures of oriental luxury and delights that have never faded; therefore among the early inquiries I made in India was the question, "Where shall we see a nautch?" Everyone said "Delhi is the place. Delhi, the ancient capital; the center of wealth, art, poetry and pleasure."

I had pictured to myself a marble court with Moorish arches, splashing fountains, mellow lights, rich rugs, divans, draperies and the voluptuous odors of sandal wood and attar of roses; and myself sitting cross-legged on a divan, smoking a hookah, whatever that is, with rose water in the bowl, while slender beauties in gauzy draperies danced before me on silken rugs to the tinkle of castanets, the tremulous cadences of the lute and the soft tones of the lyre, as they did before Solomon and Shah Jehan. In fact, I had imagined myself a Great Mogul, or an oil painting.

At last I saw the nautch. My curiosity was satisfied, but my soul was not. It is sad to lose our illusions, the most beautiful and perfect things we ever possess; and why we should ever want to is one of the fifty-seven mysteries of life.

Arrangements having been made several days in advance for so important an event, we were ushered into a room furnished with the most complete barrenness. No, the room was not completely barren, for besides the European chairs, there were European chromos on the wall showing some highly colored horse races, and a lithograph giving us the cheering intelligence that "Splittz Beer is Best." In addition there was considerable bona-fide Asiatic dirt.

Ranged against the opposite wall were seven native musicians with strange instruments and an English concertina. When the music began, two girls appeared and lifted up their voices in song. They were wonderfully and voluminously appareled. They wore blue satin waists with long sleeves embroidered in gold. Heavy skirts of cloth of gold, very full, reached to their ankles. The feet were bare, but were loaded with silver anklets and toe rings too numerous to count. Their heads and necks were roped with near-pearls and other jewels of more or less value. A shawl with golden fringe was twisted about the body, a corner of which was occasionally thrown coquettishly over the head. I had not seen so many clothes in all India. After the dance we saw these grand clothes being carefully folded and laid away, and the dancers went ·out into the street, dressed in the usual native costume consisting of a skirt that is too short at the top, and a bust-supporting jacket that is too short at the bottom, thus leaving exposed a generous expanse of bare stomach.

As I said before, they lifted up their voices in song. The song was not so bad, although we had no idea what it was about, but it seemed to possess the wild passionate thrill of an oriental love song. It had odd little quavers at the end of the measures, and considerable rhythm and swing. When they clasped their hands and rolled up their eyes, it was plain enough to me that they were making love, and I was enjoying it as such until the interpreter explained they were charming snakes.

Street Fashions.

Then they danced the "Thread-Making Dance" in which they carded imaginary wool, spun and twisted imaginary thread and made an imaginary garment.

These nautch girls might be called pretty, with their round young faces, raven hair, rich dark complexions and languishing eyes, were it not for the betel nut habit. The crushed betel nuts were placed between two green leaves, with slaked lime for flavoring, and stowed away in their mouths in prodigious quantity to be vigorously chewed during the dancing, and shuttled about during the singing. Betel nut chewing may be well enough in its place, as there is said to be a place for everything, and, according to the Philosopher, a hot one for some, but it is unromantic in dancing girls. It is diverting, for it stains their teeth a dark red, the interior of their mouths black, and leaves high water marks about their lips and the trail of accidental overflows on their shapely chins.

One girl fascinated me. She seemed to open her face in song, and as I gazed into the black abyss, I wondered if the mass, she was so skillfully shuttling about to give the song half a chance to escape, would be lost to control and drop into her larnyx, complet-

ing the strangulation, or whether it would
safely slip down her gullet and be happily
"Lost to sight if not to memory dear."

The nautch dances were a series of postur-
ings, attempts at dramatic expression, and
while not lacking in grace, were, to us,
ridiculous and monotonous. Doubtless they
appeal to the oriental mind. They must do
so; for they are the steady entertainment of
millions of Indians, and have been for thousands of years.

At last garlands of fragrant white flowers
were hung about our necks, and the entertainment was over.

As we passed out into the night through
the court-yard, we experienced the ordinary
odors of the Orient. It was not the sensu-
ous perfume of my boyhood fancy, but the
pungent emanations of goats, which according to oriental custom, pass their nights inside the house.

CHAPTER XXXIII.

JAIPUR AND THE RAJPUTS.

It is a tiresome ride over the burning, sandy plain from Delhi to Jaipur, the capital of Rajputana, one of the few native states remaining nominally independent of the English. It is a vast, parched plain from which the sunlight is reflected in a dazzling glare. The car windows are provided with smoked glass, but the penetrating dust is beyond the control of man.

This part of India is the home of famine. Occasionally we passed a green plot of ground watered by a government irrigating canal, or well, from which water for irrigating is hoisted in leather buckets by oxen. It is said water may be found almost anywhere at no great depth, but rather than dig a well on land owned by the government, which takes most of the produce, the Hindoo lies down in the sun and sleeps and starves. The Indian dearly loves the sun. It is the only thing he enjoys that he gets much of.

Here is an opportunity for the American well-driver and the wind-mill salesman, or would be if the Hindoo was commanded to

buy, and had the money to pay. He has
been governed so much that he does little he
is not commanded to do.

There is an emaciated crowd of beggars at
every railroad station. The country is full
of pigeons. They walk the streets and flock
on the roofs, but before a Hindoo will eat
meat he will starve. His religious and his
caste principles are stronger than his desire
for life. The Hindoo is the easiest "dier"
in the world. There is no humor in his life.
It is a grim struggle and full of trouble. He
bows before whichever of the malevolent
Gods his fathers did, bathes in the sacred
rivers, follows the inexorable custom of his
caste, lives until he dies,—and the mourning
is brief. He carves a hideous idol, puts it in
a temple and worships it as a God, or the
symbol of a God, according to his intelligence. The Mohammedan conqueror lifts
his battle-axe and smites the idol, saying,
"There is no God but God. No images must
be made, for God is a spirit and must be wor-
shiped in spirit." The Christian comes,
and holding aloft the crucifix, tells the beautiful story of love, redemption and salvation;
but the Hindoo can no more understand the
beatitudes of Christianity than we can com-

The Hindoo's Last Ceremonial—the Burning Gaut.

prehend the gloomy terrors of Brahmanism; and so, while the efforts of our earnest missionaries are great, and their hopes are high, the results are a little discouraging.

Though caste is undoubtedly a barrier to progress, it has its advocates. A very intelligent Englishman, long resident in India, explained to us that caste, although cruel and tyrannous, is really an advantage to the country, as its laws tend to keep the immense population in order and discipline. It has served well each conqueror of India through all ages. It would be a bad thing for England or any other reigning power if caste was abrogated and all men were considered equal, free and irresponsible to the higher caste. Anarchy would result. English rule adapts itself to the observation, protection and etiquette of caste. Although a Hindoo beggar might consider his cup defiled if the English Viceroy should drink from it, the English statesman says "It is well; so be it."

And thus we see the anomaly of the English, as a political body, defending caste and sending their oldest sons as soldiers to fight for it, and the English, as a religious body, sending their younger sons as missionaries to destroy it by the introduction of Christianity.

It seemed that since Shanghai we had been traveling through a modified England, but in Jaipur, the capital of the independent state of Rajputana, we were at last away from the shadow of the English flag, if not away from its influence.

Rajputana has its Maharajah, who sits in his harem, rides his elephants, parts his whiskers in the middle, and otherwise conducts himself as a progressive and satisfactory monarch. But he wisely listens to the voice of the English representative, who is at his right hand to give such advice as may seem good to the uncrowned English despot who resides in the Vice-regal palace in Calcutta. By following that advice as the will of heaven, he is able to continue the enjoyment of his elephants, his French chandeliers, his wives, his many dancing girls, and his three hundred assorted beauties of the harem. He paves the streets, builds industrial schools, dispenses grain to his starving subjects, names a museum Albert Memorial, paints "Welcome" on a hillside in white kalsomine, and sent an elephant to take our party to his old palace at Amber.

The last item alone shows he is a first-rate king.

Street Scene.

CHAPTER XXXIV.

A TRIP TO AMBER, AND AN ELEPHANT RIDE.

The eleven-mile ride to the deserted palace of Amber was in three chapters, carriage, ox-cart and elephant. During the first chapter we passed acres of prickly pears. This vindictive vegetable may be very well for hedges, but as a regular crop it is a failure. There are thickets of them occupying the deserted gardens of suburban villas of graceful Saracenic architecture, which have long been abandoned by the owners to the doves and crows. Wild monkeys scampered about their roofs and commented on our appearance as we passed.

When the road became bad and the country hilly we changed to a bullock cart. It had no springs, but a good deal of green canopy. We sat cross-legged in the native fashion. The white oxen were very deliberate. They stopped so frequently, and looked back so reproachfully that I got off and walked. We climbed a narrow, desolate valley between rocky hills crowned with the battlements of the ancient palace. Passing through a gate whose crumbling wooden doors bristled with iron spikes, we saw the royal elephant awaiting us before the "Amber Rest House."

We had luncheon on the veranda. Before us was a narrow valley holding a glassy pond where ducks were swimming. In the water many storks were standing on one leg.* A few natives were performing their abolutions and washing their clothes on the sandy shore. Across the pond rose a hill. A road zigzagged up its side to the castle, a marble palace on grey sandstone foundations. Still higher on the crest of the hill frowned the red sandstone fortress of the Rajput monarchs of four hundred years ago.

The road before our veranda had once thronged with the nobles of a gay court. Here came in triumph the conquerors of Delhi, but now there came a different retinue, a sorry company of thin-shanked, starving natives with a flock of children. There is no race suicide in India, even in time of famine.

These people respectfully touched their forehead and lips and rubbed their wind-distended stomachs in token of their need,

---

* That is, one leg for each stork. It is a foolish habit anyway.—*G. W. C.*

murmuring the while that we were their fathers, their mothers, their brothers, their masters and their protectors. A few coppers made them happy.

And then came another class of beggars, the monkeys. They looked better nourished than the Hindoos and appeared happier. Wild animals are not afraid in India, because the Hindoos do not frighten or harm them. Even tigers are sociable—and very fond of the Hindoos. These monkeys came to us without fear and helped themselves to food from our hands. If they found a hand empty they gave it a slap and chattered angrily.

Some wild peacocks, also scenting food, came out of the thickets to watch the proceedings from a respectable distance.

A stone-laden camel strode by, led by a Hindoo, who salaamed respectfully. We knew by the mark on his forehead he was a worshiper of Sheva. The camel had a drooping under lip, and surveyed us with a stare of contemptuous hauteur.

The royal elephant in the meantime had been breakfasting off a pile of tree branches, that looked more suitable for a stove than an elephant. As he picked it over hunting for tender twigs, he seemed to say, "I eat this 'breakfast food,' not because I like it, but because my doctor recommends it." He was not a prosperous-looking elephant. His skin was too loose. But the Rajah had sent him expressly for us as he had for numerous other chance travelers, and will continue to do on request, if the elephant holds together, which on account of his generally moth-eaten appearance is doubtful. He was a dilapidated and tumbled-down elephant with one tusk and the rheumatism. On his back was a howdah or "howdahdo," as the Philosopher called it.

The mahout talked to him in elephant and prodded him in the neck. This seemed a good deal of liberty to take with an elephant, but he came down laboriously, trumpeting a protest. We climbed to his back by means of a ladder and he rose, one end at a time, rocking like a boat. Thus perched high above the earth we bobbed along and tried to adjust ourselves to the rolls and bumps of elephant gait. The Philosopher walked back, but I being both brave and lazy, returned via elephant. Mark Twain said he could easily learn to prefer an elephant to any other vehicle, but the Philosopher would prefer a goat.

He Was a Dilapidated and Tumble-Down Elephant with one Tusk and the Rheumatism.

The interior of the palace is not equal to the peerless palaces of Delhi or Agra, or even to the imposing ruins of Futtehpore-Sikree. There is a many-pillared marble hall of audience, and some rooms with thousands of tiny mirrors set in the stucco walls and ceilings. The light came through screens of marble filigree instead of glazed windows, and there were many niches in the walls for lamps to be placed behind colored glass. Here were the only old art windows we had thus far seen in India. They represent scenes from Hindoo mythology, and have strikingly brilliant and beautiful reds, blues and greens. They are not fragments leaded together, but immense single panes, hand-painted, with the colors burned in.

From the pavilions on the roof there was a comprehensive panorama of the deserted city. In the gardens no foliage shaded the marble walks, and in the fountains birds could find no drink. Away in the distance, through a cleft in the castellated hills, was the glimmering white sand of the desert slowly filling in upon deserted and desolate Amber.

CHAPTER XXXV.

BOMBAY—THE CAVES OF ELEPHANTA.

From the veranda in front of my window in the hotel I looked out upon a continuous pageant of oriental life. There were many nations in the Indias before the British conquest. I think they were all represented in the procession that passed in the street, and besides there were representatives from nearly every other people in Europe, Asia and Africa. Across the street was a park in the very center of the city. In the grassy shade native children, dressed like cupids without the quiver, romped and laughed in the way of children the world over. Above the billowy green of the tree tops rose the familiar Gothic of the English church.

In the shade of the park trees, the street entertainers held continuous performances. One Hindoo sat on his heels and rattled a gourd to attract attention. With him were two grave monkeys and a goat. The monkeys would turn somersaults and go through the manual of arms; and the goat would walk a globe for a modest consideration.

202

Nearby was a snake charmer. He carried a bag of snakes and led a mongoose by a cord. He untied his bag and played a few weird notes on a reed; a snake came out, and coiling, inflated its hood. It was a cobra. His part of the entertainment was to fight the mongoose. A mongoose resembles a small coon. He has thick brown fur, beady, red eyes and a dissipated nose. He is a sort of thug among the snakes. He has a perpetual grouch and kills for the pleasure,—when he does not get himself swallowed, as sometimes happens.

The Parsees are a noticeable people on the streets. They are descendants of the ancient Persians, and still follow the religion of Zoroaster, or fire worship, as it is sometimes called. In Bombay they are the leaders in business, finance, education and philanthropy. They live in handsome mansions on Malabar Hill, and in the afternoon their victorias may be seen among the fashionable throng on the Apollo Bunder Boulevard. Their women wrap themselves in yards of sheeny, thin silks after the Greek fashion. The men wear a peculiar hat, resembling a rimless silk hat with the rear dented in—a hat which if seen on Broadway, would lay

its wearer open to the suspicion of having
had a night out with the boys.

The Parsees believe the elements, fire,
water and earth, to be sacred, and should not
be defiled by contact with the dead. Therefore they place their dead on towers called
"Towers of Silence" for the vultures to devour.

A sail across the bay to the Caves of Elephanta brought us again to a shrine of ancient India. This rock-hewn temple is one
of many of the kind in India and Ceylon.
The images and the columns were much dam-
aged by the cannon of the Portuguese who
took that means to teach the Golden Rule.
The Hindoo name is "The Hill of Purifica-
tion." The word Elephanta was adopted
by the Portuguese on account of the colossal
stone elephants that stood before the entrance. These ruins, and the native temples
in India generally, are now carefully guarded
and protected by the Anglo-Indian government, in sharp contrast with the iconoclastic
fury of the Portuguese.

Bombay, like Calcutta, is so Europeanized,
that having seen the real India of the interior,
there is little to hold the traveler beyond the
next sailing day. Consequently we were soon

again upon the placid waters of the Indian Ocean.

Romance and beauty there is in plenty in India, but it is so deeply buried in degradation and desolation that it does not appear at first glance. In time, when the unpleasant things have been somewhat obscured by a merciful forgetfulness, the poetry and subtle charm peep through the picture, and ever after we treasure the memories of the magnificent East,—the land of great things, good and bad,—the cradle of the human race.

CHAPTER XXXVI.

THE INDIAN OCEAN, AND THE RED SEA.

The Indian Ocean in winter is an ideal sea for the smooth-water sailor. We remembered the tossing, cold North Pacific with a shudder. During the days the passengers played shuffle-board, quoits, poker and other deck games, or read and dozed in steamer chairs. In the star-lit evenings there were concerts, dances, flirtations and lemon squashes to suit everyone. The shadowy fore-deck, or flirtation parlor, as the Philosopher called it, was a favorite retreat for young couples to study the sparkling phosphorescence of the waters as they curled away from the prow.

In the early morning the sailors hosed down the decks. Then the men passengers went up in their pajamas and walked in their bare feet on the cool, damp deck, took deep breaths of the delicious air, drank their coffee, and envied the Lascar sailors who can go all day in bare feet and pajamas and sail such an ocean as long as they live. For days we saw no ships,—nothing but sea, and sky, and horizon, and the ruffled waters of our wake.

At Aden it rained. This is not mentioned as news, but as a marvel, for Aden is supposed to be the driest place on earth. It appeared like a mammoth ash heap. Somali boys came alongside and dived for coins. Negroes from Somaliland on the African coast, and Arabs from Aden clambered on deck to sell their ostrich plumes, eggs, baskets and other curios, but they were ordered off, and the hose turned on them to accelerate their departure.

As we drew towards the northern end of the Red Sea, a brown irregular line rose on the eastern horizon, and steadily grew until the Sinaitic range of mountains spread their barren and ragged outlines against the turquois blue of the Arabian sky.

Mount Sinai, the mountain of the law, can be seen, so the mate said, for a few minutes at a certain point of the course, but like the proverbial golden opportunity, it is easily missed. The eastern shore stretched away in hillocks of drifting sand to the sun-baked mountains that are rocky and torn, like volcanoes long burned out, and barren as the surface of the moon.

Near Suez there is an oasis, a patch of green and a few trees on the sandy plain.

This is Moses' Well, the place where Moses smote the rock and the water came forth, and behold it was bitter. The water is still bitter. It is now an Egyptian quarantine station, a bulwark for Europe against the plagues of India. Some of our fellow passengers who have been detained there said the accommodations have not improved since Moses' time. Opposite the spring is the place in the Red Sea where Moses divided the waters, and the children of Israel passed over, dry shod, but Pharaoh's host was swallowed up. The mate said sailors often bring up on their anchors, swords, muskets, chariot wheels and things; but he did not have any for souvenirs just at that time.

Moses divided the sea, but De Lesseps divided the land. When we sat at dinner in the saloon while steaming through the Suez Canal, we could look through the port holes on either side and see nothing but sandy desert. We went through the canal in sixteen hours. During the night our search-lights enabled us to proceed at the same speed as in the day. I was informed the toll for our ship amounted to ten thousand dollars, which seemed incredible.

CHAPTER XXXVII.

HOW WE BROKE INTO EGYPT—THE REWARD
OF HONESTY.

Port Said is supposed to be the wickedest city of its size in the world. It looked innocent enough with the shields of the various national consulates displayed from buildings along the water front. In the town the principal business seemed to be the selling of curios and antiques which looked suspiciously new.

Here we disembarked for Cairo, but first we had to go to the quarantine station. The very sound of the word "quarantine" filled us with shivers of dread, and forebodings of evil, for we had come from plague-infested India, and had heard uncanny tales of Moses' Well, the quarantine pen and other Egyptian health resorts.

The passengers for Egypt and their baggage, were loaded into boats, and the flotilla, tied together like canal boats, was towed by a hysterical tug up the canal a mile to the dreaded quarantine station. A dragoman had been sent to help us through, and he stood in the prow of the boat like Washington crossing the Delaware. He was to be our interpreter and protector, and when we looked upon him we were reassured, for he had a long cimeter, a fierce red face, and awe-inspiring clothing. He wore a blue Turkish jacket wonderfully embroidered in gold braid, and Turkey red cotton trousers with a lamentable absence of fit. They apparently were cut to fit a pear. Their voluminous folds were gathered around the ankles, but there was an appalling redundancy of seat which trailed in a pouch between his feet like the generous stomach of a goose that had overlaid itself. On the back of his head was a red fez with a flame of a tassel that snapped with the energy of his gesticulation. He assured us we were not to be detained, but only baked, boiled, steamed and sterilized for the public safety.

The quarantine station proved to be a dock with a corrugated iron roof and a terrifying machine on wheels like an ancient locomotive. Into its fiery furnace an Arab was shoveling coal. Above was an oven about the size of a tourist, and from it came the sound of escaping steam. That was the sterilization plant and they were ready for us. Some of us were nervous. The prospect for baked tourist was good. The native boys who came with us jumped overboard and escaped.

A wordy war was going on between our dragoman and the Egyptian health officer. They talked in Egyptian and with both hands. It was plain they were very angry and swearing frightfully. What would we do without our brave defender! Finally he turned to us smiling and said:

"It is all right; all they want is your soiled linen."

Ladies who had looked bravely into the fiery furnace turned pale with dismay. They gazed at one another, but no one moved. They were paralyzed with fear.

Cotton bags to receive the linen were handed around. The Philosopher from Philadelphia, being like all Philadelphians, strictly honest, opened his trunk and stuffed in his entire laundry. Another man compromised with his conscience by hesitatingly opening his handbag and surreptitiously extracting a suit of pajamas which he turned over to the strong arm of the law.

In the midst of this turmoil, an experienced traveler, being a diplomat, if not worse, denied that he had any soiled linen whatsoever.

Since India he had not even changed his shirt. It was a brave thing to say, but it seemed to go. It appeared natural enough to the Egyptians. They understood it. He was excused. Then a strange thing happened. Not another passenger would confess to the possession of a scrap of soiled linen, so the proceedings came to an abrupt termination.

The laundry was returned dripping wet and steaming hot to the two honest men; and then they had the reward for their honesty. They were required to pay a shilling for each article, which proved quite a tax on the very honest man—the Philosopher from Philadelphia, who had given his all in the laundry list. He thought they should iron it for that amount.

But our troubles were not over. We still had to run the gauntlet at the custom house before we could go up into Egypt land. We were towed to another dock, and our luggage dumped on the platform where the Egyptian custom officers lay in wait for us.

However, they seemed remarkably mild and confiding for custom officers, for they were rapidly putting their chalk marks on the baggage of the entire shipload of passengers as they hurried to the train. There was no annoyance, no trouble in sight. It was a remarkably cheerful place—for a custom house. Our dragoman took possession of our keys, and remarked with a falling inflex-ion, as an eyelid slowly drooped, "No duti-able goods, I suppose."

It was a mistake to have taken the Phi-losopher into the custom house at all. He should have been safely put aboard the train with a guide book and a cigar. It is strange how the habit of honesty will grow on a person. At first it may be indulged in as a mild recreation or dissipation, but the sen-sation is so strange and enticing that the habit grows until the victim becomes hope-lessly honest and in no condition to be trusted alone in a custom house. I saw the mistake, but it was too late; he had made the fatal ad-mission that he might possibly have half a box of cigars somewhere in his trunks.

The officer was plainly astonished at such an unusual admission. He was so skeptical about it that nothing short of seeing them with his own eyes would convince him that the statement was true. He demanded to see the cigars. That required that the trunks be opened, but through some mistake, our dragoman opened the wrong trunk. It belonged to the diplomat of the quarantine station, and he was displeased about it; for there, before the astonished gaze of the officer, lay his forgotten dutiable articles—all his purchase and plunder of the "purple east"— silks, embroideries, tiger skins, and ivories. There was duty to pay, and perhaps, frightful penalties for having such a poor memory.

The diplomat explained that he was only passing through Egypt; that rather than pay heavy duties he would express the whole lot through to London.   It was no use; he had deceived the government; the government was angry and he must pay.   The officer was positive about it.   He said so in seven languages and at last in English.   Train time was approaching.   We had missed our dinner over this custom muddle and were likely to miss our train.   The diplomat capitulated to Egypt and asked for the amount of the duty.

The officer plunged an arm into one corner of the open trunk, contemplated the others from a distance, and began to figure.

"Never mind the harrowing details," said the diplomat, "give us the terrible total."

"Thirty-three piastres," declared the officer, and proceeded to chalk all our trunks.

The diplomat was delighted, for thirty-three piastres are equivalent to only $1.65 in real money.

As our dragoman got him into the difficulty he volunteered to help him out. "If you will all go on the train," he said, "I will attend to this business."

We were well toward Cairo when the dragoman appeared to return our keys and report the trunks were on board. As the diplomat received his keys he said, "I will settle with you for the duties you paid."

"I did not pay the duties," declared the dragoman.

"Neither did I," said the diplomat.

"Neither did I," echoed the Philosopher.

"But who did?"

"At any rate my conscience is clear," said the Philosopher. "It was my duty to declare, and their duty to collect. I have observed that after all, honesty is the best policy—if you are caught at it."

CHAPTER XXXVIII.

PORT SAID TO CAIRO.

The ride from Port Said to Cairo is full of interest. Even the brown desert has a charm because it is so frankly and thoroughly a desert. Over that course through which we rolled so rapidly and comfortably in palace cars, have passed the hosts of conquering armies.

If the sands could speak, they could tell of conquerors, whose names were forgotten before history was carved on stone. They could tell of Rameses and his triumph; of the children of Israel brought captives in chains; of Moses, Aaron and David; of the fleeing Israelites, and the pursuing hosts of Pharaoh; perhaps of the Queen of Sheba journeying from her Arabian capital; of Cambyses the Persian; Alexander the Great; of the humble Mary and Joseph fleeing into Egypt with the Christ child; of Julius Caesar; and of Napoleon pressing on to the seige of Jaffa, eager with ambition to found an Asiatic Empire, and repeat the conquests of Tamerlane. Perhaps if his plans had not miscarried, Europe would have been spared that carnival of blood during his revival of the Empire of Charlemagne.

The peculiar natural conditions of the Nile valley were especially favorable for the early development of civilization. Upon the annual inundation of the valley depended the prosperity of the people. This fact, together with the mystery of its source, caused it to be invested with sanctity, and considered with reverence by the early Egyptians. On account of the great fertility of the soil, a dense population could be supported. The necessity of controlling the currents, and the building of irrigating canals, led to the development of the science of engineering. As the annual inundation obliterated the boundaries between the individual holdings, it became necessary to re-survey boundaries and keep permanent records. This developed the science of surveying and mathematics. To settle the disputes that would naturally arise, courts were established, and fixed rules, or laws, adopted. This developed a judicial system. To foretell the dates when inundations would occur, the phases of the moon and the constellations of the starry heavens were observed. Thus calendars were tabulated and the study of astronomy was fostered. To record all these facts a system of written characters became necessary, and the priesthood, which was the learned class, evolved the written language known as hieroglyphics. For economy and convenience, a plant that grows plentifully in the lower Nile was used to make a surface upon which to write. That plant was the papyrus and the product was called paper. In this manner was laid the foundation of the political, legal, social and scientific system which we call civilization.

Towards evening we saw a green valley ahead, and the glimmer of the waters of "Father Nile." Beyond was the Libyan desert, and on its edge were three pyramids like geometrical blocks. At last we were in Egypt, —the land of the lotus and papyrus, and the spell of its mystery was upon us.

CHAPTER XXXIX.

At Cairo the orient and the occident meet, but do not blend. Each preserves its own characteristics. In the great hotels may be found European luxury to satisfy the most exacting of the wealthy tourists who find in the sunlight of Egypt refuge from the rigors of northern winters.

Here the traveler may ride in a victoria or an automobile. If he prefers the oriental mode of rapid transit he may stride the diminutive donkey, some of which are so small they have been known to walk out from between the legs of a particularly tall tourist when he inadvertently rested his feet upon the ground. Or he may perch upon the apex of a camel and be shaken and groaned at by that supercilious and over-praised "ship of the desert."

If he pleases the tourist may sail up the Nile in a dahabeah to Abydos, Thebes, Karnak, and Philae. Day after day he may laze in his hammock under deck awnings, and

dream of the glory of Egypt that has depart-
ed. He may bask in the warm sunlight and
breathe the pure air of the desert. He may
watch the passing dahabeahs propelled by
lanteen sails or by men with long sweeps as
in the time of Cleopatra. He may see the
descendants of the ancient Egyptians working at the shadoofs, or well sweeps, with
leathern buckets by which water is raised
from the Nile to the irrigating ditches. He
may see barren deserts, brown hills, green
meadows, palm groves, mud villages, and the
endless procession of bare-footed women in
flowing robes of blue cotton, coming to the
bank, and carrying away urns of water on
their heads. At his pleasure the tourist may
moor his dahabeah at the bank and visit
the native market places. He will see the
wild Bedouins of the desert and the strange
people from darkest Africa. He may see
their native dances and be present at their
festivals. He may explore ruined temples
and subterranean tombs, and purchase scara-
bees, statuettes and antiquities that may have
been dragged from the tomb of a king which
had been concealed in the hills for five thousand years, or may have been made in Ger-
many last month.

Egyptian Women Carrying Water from the Nile.

Cairo is only an upstart city of a thousand years old,—a mere yesterday in Egypt. It was built by the Arabian conqueror on the ruins of New Babylon which had been founded by Cambyses the Babylonian. It contains the purest examples of Saracenic architecture, and is the center of education and culture of the Moslem world. In a few minutes walk from the luxurious hotels one may find quarters of old Cairo, where the Arabian civilization is hardly scratched. It is as it was hundreds of years ago.

The traveler soon gets accustomed to seeing mosques, for one is always in sight. We naturally dropped into them as we did into the temples of Japan, and the tombs in India.

There is nothing more pleasing in architecture than a Saracenic arch, nothing so graceful as a minaret. The heavy Roman, the ornate Renaissance and the classic Greek command respect and admiration, but they are the prose of architecture while the light and airy Saracenic is the poetry. The Saracenes built not so much to defy time and earthquakes, as to please the eye and cheer the heart. The style suggests happiness, song and laughter, the splashing of fountains and the perfume of flowers. It is not merely the proportions that please but the exquisite art of the decorative finish. If you enter a mosque and behold the rich mellow tints of the tiles in the wall; the intricate arabesque of the ceilings; the brilliant mosaics of the pulpit and prayer niche, with their geometrical patterns in ivory, ebony, jasper, and mother-of-pearl, you will say with the Moslem, "Here I will rest awhile and be content."

The mosques are always open. In them are no images, no pictures, no seats; but the true believers are always coming and going. The Arab with his fine physique, his flowing robes and dignified turban commands respect; he is picturesque withal and looks his best in a mosque. He is becoming to the architecture and they combine to make the picture as it should be.

The religion of Islam requires five things absolutely: prayer five times every day; the observation of bodily cleanliness; the pilgrimage to Mecca; the bestowal of alms on the poor; and the keeping of the fast of Ramadan, during which for forty days no food whatever must pass the lips between sunrise and sunset. All alcoholic liquors are strictly forbidden by Mohammed.

When a follower of the Prophet desires

to do a good act, he builds a mosque and set-
tles upon it an endowment for its support and
maintenance. There are no regular congre-
gations; everyone may equally enjoy its advantages. If the endowment fails it gradually falls into ruin. A good many seem to
have failed in Cairo.

To a Moslem a mosque is more than a
church to be used fifty-two times a year. It
is a house of constant prayer and a place of
refuge. There he may rest and escape the
mid-day heat. There he may refresh himself
with food which he has brought, and quench
his thirst at the fountain; the poor man may
roll himself in his blanket and sleep; he may
sew on his buttons and repair his clothing; he
may read his book or study the Koran.

From a balcony encircling a slender minaret, one frequently hears the voice of the
Muezzin calling the faithful to prayer. Five
times a day he walks around the balcony
chanting the familiar cry, "Allah Akbar; Allah Akbar; la Allah ill' Allah; Heyya alas-
salah." "God is great; God is great; there
is no God but God, and Mohammed is his
prophet; Come to prayer."

The followers of the prophet enter the
court and at the fountain wash their feet,

faces, and mouths. They enter the mosque barefooted, leaving their sandals at the door. Facing the prayer niche, which indicates the direction of Mecca, they pray to the one God —which in the Arabic language is called Allah, and in Hebrew is called Jehovah. The God of Moses and Aaron; the God of the Jew and of the Christian.

Unbelievers in the Prophet are welcome to enter and remain as long as they like, the only requirement being their shoes must be covered by mosque slippers, which are furnished at the door.

The Mohammedans come very near to following the injunction "Pray without ceasing." No matter what the work or business on hand may be, the Moslem, who follows the injunction of the Prophet, interrupts it five times a day long enough to turn his face toward Mecca and say a prayer. It is no strange sight to see a laborer throw down his tools; devote a few moments to his religious duty, then resume with renewed energy to make up for lost time. The merchant prays in his booth, the sailor on the deck of his boat; even my donkey boy ceased calling maledictions on the head of my donkey, "Yankee Doodle," long enough to mumble a prayer which I hope was a plea for forgiveness.

Our dragoman told the Philosopher from Philadelphia, that Mohammedism is still growing in Asia and Africa. He recited some of the Koran, declaring that in time all the world would become followers of the Prophet. I think he was trying to convert Phil, but the Philosopher thought such a religion would be inconvenient for every day use, and that it would never become popular in America.

"Imagine," he said, "the bulls and bears of Wall Street, the people in the department stores, or even the street car conductors, or the icemen interrupting their pursuit of the almighty dollar, five times a day—to pray. How could a religion become popular which requires a six weeks' ride on the hump of a camel across a burning desert to worship before a shrine of Mohammed in Mecca, when there is a shrine of chance wide open in Saratoga; a shrine of beauty on the sands of Atlantic City; and a shrine of Epicurus at the end of almost any automobile run? The Americans will never submit to polygamy. What chance would a man have against five mothers-in-law? Imagine the chaos that would result if that command of Mohammed prohibiting alcoholic liquors was observed. How could we manage our elections? How would we keep our army of policemen busy? How would we fill our large and commodious jails? How could we even enjoy a good dinner, or entertain our friends, the 'jolly good fellows?'"

No, Mohammedism is not suited to the strenuous life of Europe or America. Still, with all our superior civilization we can learn something of the advantages of temperate living from the Orientals.

> " When at the bowl's deep brink,
> Let the thirsty think
>   What they say in Japan,
> ' First the man takes a drink,
> Then the drink takes a drink,
>   Then the drink takes the man.' "

CHAPTER XL.

There is no better way to see Cairo than from the spine of a donkey. It is not graceful and not over-comfortable; for your donkey boy, who runs behind, will smite the beast more mightily than did Balaam; and Yankee Doodle, Bonaparte, or whatever his name may be, will cavort and trot with stiff knees until you plead for a slower pace.

The names of these donkeys are wonderfully contrived. They vary with the nationality of the employer. The shrewd donkey boys, who stand in front of the hotels, assign them names from time to time to please one and all. They are accurate guessers of nationality, and an American, no matter how English his pith helmet may be, or how many pugarees he may wind around his hat, is sure to be met with such salutations as "Please mister, mine good donkey; give you long ride; name 'George Washington,' or 'Yankee Doodle.'" But if a traveler comes along who bears the unmistakable signs of an Englishman, they will say, "Come have nice ride,

227

my donkey, name 'Prince of Wales' or
'Gladstone.' " If one appears who wears an
imperial and talks with his hands you will
hear something that sounds like, "Allez mon
chevalet; mon tres joli 'Bonaparte.' " If a
man marches out of the hotel, talking in his
throat and choking with languages, they will
cry, "Das Asel ist nicht spitzpuperi gemacht,
namen, 'Bismarck,' Hoch der Kaiser." And
all the time it will be the same jackass by the
name of Bill.

Having mounted the donkey with the most
attractive name you will see strange sights
in the native quarter. Some streets are so
narrow that only one donkey can pass at a
time, and if you should meet another donkey,
or rather if your donkey should meet another
donkey, it would be necessary for one of them
to squeeze against a doorway to allow the
other to pass. As you proceed through the
narrow streets the boy cries in Arabic, the
warning, "Take heed, fair maid;" "Beware,
O Chief," and passersby flatten themselves
against the walls. The donkey picks his way
among the crowds with almost human cau-
tion, and apologizes with his gentle eyes if
he crowds against a person.

The vendors of drinking water and lemonade carry their goods in goat skins on their backs. They jingle brass drinking bowls together, as they cry, "A drink for the thirsty —sweet water, O Chief—nectar for the faithful,—a drink in the name of Allah."

The Philosopher says, "If the custom of poetical cries for hucksters should extend to America, we may expect to hear: "Peanuts good people, sweet fruit of the sand; how beautiful are the gems of Virginia. Peanuts O, small boy," and instead of the rancous demand of a rude iceman we will hear the gentle call, "Ice, oh beautiful lady; ice for the cooler; cold butter for the biscuits; winter frost for the summer nectar, ice, oh damsel, fair."

The Arabic tongue is not only poetical in style but pleasing to the ear. Mohammed said, "I love the Arabic language because I am an Arab; because the Koran is in Arabic; and because Arabic is the language of paradise." When printed it looks like shorthand gone wrong. Our numerals are Arabic and they are shorthand when compared to the cumbersome Roman.

We visited the old university of El Azhar, the splendid. This school has been a center of Mohammedan learning for a thousand years. During the fourteenth century it is said to have had as many as twenty thousand students. Now it has perhaps five thousand. It continues to send its graduates throughout all Islam from Samarkand to Philippopolis, and Trebizond to Timbuctoo, wherever they are. It seems like an incredible distance to me.

El Azhar is conservative. Its curriculum includes the Koran, which is committed to memory, grammar, rhetoric, versification, Arabic and Persian literature, elocution, oratory, logic, mathematics, law and probably other subjects; but modern sciences and original research are sadly neglected. Tuition is free, and all students, may, if they like, sleep on the floor, eat their food, and have their heads shaven by the tonsorial artist within the courts.

The students sit upon the floor and study, bobbing their heads. This swaying of the head is a natural inclination of children the world over. Perhaps it helps to shake down the lessons on the principle of a grain hopper, but in the Mussulman it is a habit acquired by the rule that the head is to be bowed every time the word Allah is spoken. In the great court, the students sat on the pavement in groups surrounding the teachers, and as all studied aloud there was a constant hum of voices.

At one side of the court there is an open hall whose roof is supported by one hundred and eight graceful columns of granite, marble, and alabaster. Near the pulpit, two are set close together. There is a legend that only honest men can pass between them. The columns are well worn by those who have squeezed through. Our dragoman related the sad plight of a portly lady, with an hourglass figure, who got stuck between the pillars at her narrowest point, and was extricated with considerable difficulty by a lot of alarmed students. He said the legend had nothing to say about women, so the portent was unreliable.

There is a fascination about the native bazaars which draws the traveler there many times. He may roam at leisure among cool labyrinthian passages protected from the sun by gaily colored awnings. The booths are wide open to the street and often no larger than American show windows. He may see the silversmiths, the brasscutters and slipper-makers, intent upon their work in the booths where their products are offered for sale.

The merchants, in their flowing robes and turbans, have plenty of time to smoke their water-pipes, drink their black coffee and gravely converse with their neighbors.

In separate booths are displayed the rich, soft rugs of Persia; the gold and silver embroidered veils of Cairo; the metal wares of Damascus; the turquois and pearl jewelry of Arabia and the ostrich plumes and eggs of Nubia. In the booths of the perfumers are the gilded vials of attar of roses from the rose gardens of Turkey, fragrant herbs from Persia, sandalwood from India, benzoin from Siam, and myrrh and frankincense from Arabia. Their sweet odors escape from the booths and perfume the mazes of the bazaars.

At every turn is a new scene abounding with the colors which please an artist. It may be a mosque banded with red and white sandstone; a sculptured fountain of ablutions pouring forth its cooling waters; a slender white minaret against a background of a turquois sky; or perhaps, an unusually graceful mouchrabiyeh window whose intricate fretwork of cedar spindles clings to the wall like a swallow's nest.

At the further end of the bazaars is one of the mediaeval gateways in the walls of

Cairo. It is ornamented with Arabic inscriptions carved in stone. In its shadowy recesses, hung high and safe above reach, are old chains and battle-axes, reminding us of the middle ages when Islam triumphant was beating in the gates of Europe in the valley of the Danube, and on the sunny slopes of Spain. They remind us of the brave days of the Crusades, when Arabs and Turks crossed swords with Christian knights for the possession of the holy places of Palestine. Through that gate passed many a cavalcade of the Chivalry of Islam going forth in the panoply of war clad cap-a-pie in good Damascus steel, with mailed hands upon the keen swords of Toledo, and mounted on gaily caparisoned steeds of the best blood of Arabia.

CHAPTER XLI.

Sultan Saladin, who captured Jerusalem from the Crusaders, built a citadel, and within it a palace, on the slope of the Mokattam hills overlooking the city of Cairo. Mohammed Ali leveled the palace and built on its site his mosque veneered with alabaster slabs and beautified with alabaster pillars. Its great dome, and slender white minarets rise above the frowning battlements and are the most conspicuous feature of the city.

Mohammed Ali was buried in his mosque in 1849 almost on the spot where he committed one of the most terrible massacres in history. He was a progressive but ruthless man; he did great things for himself and incidentally considerable for Egypt. Although a Turk, and a Turkish viceroy, his ambition was to make Egypt a great and independent nation with realms from the Red Sea to the Atlantic, and from the Mediterranean to the source of the Nile.

The Mamelukes were opposed to progress. They were an influential military race. Away

234

back in the thirteenth century they were a
corps of cavalry made up of slaves sold to
the Sultan of Egypt by an Asiatic Kahn.
They were intended as a body guard to over-
awe rebellious subjects, but in time they came
to own their owners. At various times they
seized the government and made their leaders sultans, and at all times were turbulent
and dictatorial.

Mohammed Ali, tiring of their opposition,
invited four hundred and fifty of their leaders
to a conference in the citadel. When they arrived, the gates were closed and all were shot
from their horses except one who spurred his
horse over the wall, falling what appears a
hundred feet, and fled, miraculously escaping
with his life. At the same time a general
slaughter of the Mamelukes was ordered
throughout Egypt. Such a carnival of murder followed as had not been witnessed in
Egypt since the slaughter of the first born.
After that Mohammed Ali developed his
plans unhindered.

From the citadel can be seen a panorama
of Cairo which can never be forgotten. The
best time to see it is at sunset when the peculiar azure and golden haze of Egypt add
their magical charm to the picture. Nearby

are the half ruined tombs of the Mameluke
Sultans, clustered upon the desert sand at the
foot of the Mokattam hills. Stretching away
to the north and south is the City of Cairo,
thickly dotted with the swelling domes and
tapering minarets of mosques. Midway of
the valley flows the Nile. Its shining course
can be traced far up and down, and on its
surface can be seen the lateen sails of the
dahabeahs. Over beyond the green valley
is the brown waste of the Libyan desert
stretching away in sandy undulations, into
the golden haze of the distance. On the
edge of the desert, as on a platform, stand the
three pyramids of Gizeh. Their huge triangles notch the sky at the horizon, and their
sides seem turned to dull gold by the sunset.
Near the Pyramids crouches the Sphinx, gaz-
ing back at us with the mystery of the ages,
as it gazed back upon Moses, Joseph, Mary,
and the sacred child, and St. Mark, who established the Christian church among the
Egyptians; as it gazed upon Rameses, Pharaoh, Cambyses, Julius Caesar, Cleopatra,
Saladin and Napoleon; and as it will gaze
upon ages yet unborn.

How paragraphs rush to the pen and strive
to be free, but I forbear, for who can compre-

A Vigil of Six Thousand Years.

hend six thousand years of the past? Who can conceive of the possibilities of six thousand years of the future?

CHAPTER XLII.

THE PYRAMIDS—THE PHILOSOPHER MAKES
SOME DISCOVERIES.

The drive to the pyramids is across the
Nile bridge, flanked by British lions, and
along a roadway embanked above the line of
inundation and shaded by lubbuk trees. On
the road we met many donkeys loaded with
vegetables for the city markets, and camels
almost enveloped in their load of green grass
destined for fodder for "Yankee Doodle,"
"Bismarck," "Bonaparte" and the other donkeys with high sounding names that carry the
tourists about Cairo. We met the Bedouins
of the desert with long rifles across their
knees, mounted on spirited horses. Behind
them came camels shambling along under
their loads of Bedouin women, veiled and
heavily draped in black.

There were also automobiles and trolley
cars, but we ignored them, and mentally
placarded them with the signs worn by the
"supers" in the Japanese plays when they are
to be considered invisible. They have no

place in the memory picture which I wish to preserve.

As we drew nearer the Pyramids, our respect for them increased. As their bulk grew larger in the perspective they grew in impressiveness. When, at length, our carriage halted before the Great Pyramid, it seemed a colossal stone pile, a mountain of masonry. It has served as a stone quarry for the buildings of Cairo with little more than scratching the surface. It has been robbed of the casing of polished granite which was covered with hieroglyphics. Its secret chambers have been discovered, and the mummy of its royal builder dragged into the light much against his wish, but the pyramid remains to the ages the most stupendous structure erected by man.

Its base is more than an eighth of a mile square. Its apex is over a twelfth of a mile high, and its covers thirteen acres. The secret passage to the interior was found on the thirteenth layer of stones, and the average height of each block of stone is nearly four feet. As an evidence of the mathematical and astronomical knowledge possessed by their builders, it is curious to note that the sides exactly correspond with the cardinal points of the compass, yet at that early day the compass had not been invented. The diagonal of the Great Pyramid projected, forms the diagonal of the second pyramid in the group. The narrow secret passage is built at the correct angle to observe the pole-star from the center of the pyramid at a certain day in the year. The stone used was brought from a great distance on the other side of the Nile, and was probably transported by barges at high water, or by canals built for the purpose. All of these facts are comforting to know.

At present the Pyramids are owned by Bedouins who for a fee will pull and push the tourist to the apex, and for another fee will push him down again. Whether the charge is so much per person, or so much per pound, I did not learn, but the Philosopher discovered it was so much per push, for he unknowingly had an extra pusher, and the Sheik reminded him of it when he came to settle.

These Bedouins have camels to rent for the ride to the Sphinx. After the ride, which consisted of a boost, a groan, a jounce, and a get-off, the Philosopher proceeded to lead away the animal, thinking he had bought it; but the Sheik sent a dozen Bedouins to bring

On the Road to the Pyramids.

it back and collected a double fee for wearing out his camel without a permit.

The Sphinx, which is carved out of the bed-rock of the plateau, has been subjected to gross indignities. The winds have buried its body with desert sands, which, however, have been partially removed. Its face has been used as a target for cannon practice with the result that it has lost the greater part of its nose, and has acquired a hare-lip. Its beard, for it was originally the likeness of a gentleman known as Amenemhet III, has been plucked and carted away to the British Museum. But in spite of all these insults it has never spoken except once when Ralph Waldo Emerson stood before it, and several persons distinctly heard it say, "You're an-other."

CHAPTER XLIII.

THE DERVISHES.

Once a week the "Howling Dervishes" and the "Whirling Dervishes" hold services in their respective mosques. "The public are cordially invited to attend." If the dragoman has provided a carriage with fast horses it is possible to see both in one afternoon. These dervishes are a Mohammedan sect sometimes called fanatics.

We went first to the "Howling Dervishes," and found a throng of spectators, native and foreign, grouped around a court in the center of which was an elevated platform under a grape trellis. On the platform stood a circle of dervishes repeating in unison with much explosive vehemence, "La Allah ill' Allah." Every time they said "Allah" they violently bowed their heads. The tempo set by the leader gradually increased and the bobbing of their heads became more energetic until their entire bodies swung backward and forward with wonderful rapidity. There was one who wore no turban and his long hair fairly snapped like a whip lash, as it flew back and forth with his violent exercise. It seemed that they would never tire, or that they would fall from exhaustion. After some minutes, the time gradually retarded, and their movements became less violent until they were silent and still again. Again they walked around in a circle and prayed, then resumed their cries of "Allah" and began another movement in which deep and rapid breathing seemed to be the object.

One man especially interested me. It was he of the flying hair. He was perhaps twenty-eight years of age. He had a pallid, delicate complexion, sparse, curling, brown beard, and abundant wavy brown hair falling about his shoulders. His large brown eyes seemed to have no sin. The purity of his face, his devotional intensity and his spiritual expression would put any question of his sincerity to shame. He was a monk, an ascetic from Palestine.

By a fast ride we were able to see the dancing dervishes. Their mosque at first glance had an irreverent appearance. The center of the building was railed off, and inside the railing were several dervishes, each spinning like a top by himself. No one interfered with his neighbor. With closed eyes and folded

arms, their leaded skirts standing out like
round tables, they whirled until it would
seem they must drop.

. These enthusiasts endeavor to induce a
condition of ecstacy, hallucination, hypnotism, or trance, during which they see visions,
and in which their souls are freed from the
trammels of the body, and can soar to the
realms of the blessed, peep into the courts of
paradise, and commune with God. The
"Howling Dervishes" adopt the method of
violent movements of the head and deep
breathing, the effect of which is to disturb the
circulation of blood in the brain, and intoxi-
cate with an excess of oxygen. The "Whirling Dervishes" adopt the method of produc-
ing the desired condition of mind by vertigo,
induced by rapid and long whirling. The
Hindoo fakirs produce the same condition by
mere concentration of mind.

This condition of perfect subjugation of
self during which the spirit, or soul, or astral
body rises triumphant over the earthly body,
to see things unseen by ordinary mortals, is a
state desired by enthusiasts of all religions,
and accomplished in various ways. It is the
condition that makes the acceptance of mar-
tyrdom a trivial thing. Christian ascetics

have sought the same condition by fasting, prayer and meditation.

The Persian astronomer-poet, Omar Khayyam, expressed the purpose and his conclusion when he wrote, in "The Rubaiyat"

> " I sent my soul through the invisible,
>   Some letter of that after-life to spell ;—
> And by-and-by my soul returned to me,
>   And answered, ' I myself am Heaven and hell.'
> Heav'n but the vision of fulfilled desire,
> And Hell the Shadow of a Soul on fire.''

CHAPTER XLIV.

MEMPHIS—HELIOPOLIS—THE WISDOM OF THE EGYPTIANS.

The Prophet Jeremiah wrote, "Noph, (Memphis) shall be waste and desolate without an inhabitant." His prophecy has literally been fulfilled. There is nothing now to mark the ancient metropolis of lower Egypt but the fallen statues of Rameses II, the Pharaoh of the oppression, which stood before the Temple of Ptah.

That temple was the most important in Egypt, but its stones have been removed for the building of Cairo, and nothing now remains but the gigantic granite statue, forty-two feet high, of Rameses II and the mummies in the tombs of Sakkara on the edge of the desert. In the worship and ceremonials of the ancient Egyptians, bulls were employed. They were considered sacred to Apis, and when they died they were mummified and placed in the subterranean tombs connected with the temples in granite sarcophagi, some of which weight sixty-five tons.

It is an interesting problem how such enor-

mous weights as these sarcophagi, the obe-
lisks, and the mammoth statues, were transported hundreds of miles from their quarries
in upper Egypt. The statue of Rameses in
the Rameseum in Thebes, carved from a single block of red granite, stood fifty-five feet
and is estimated to have weighed eight hundred and eighty-seven tons. The quarrying
and cutting of these blocks were done with
tools of tempered copper, some of which
have been found; but the secret of tempering
copper is one of the lost arts, although known
to the North American Aborigines.

In the northern suburbs of Cairo is the
site of the ancient City of Heliopolis, the
sacred City of the Temple of the Sun,—the
"On" of the forty-first chapter of Genesis.
This was a center of learning in ancient
Egypt—a sort of university town. Moses
was a student there, and became learned in all
the wisdom of the Egyptians. Herodotus,
Plato and Strabo, journeyed there to study
philosophy and history. Dionysius, an Egyptian astronomer at Heliopolis, recorded a
darkness or eclipse on the date of the cruci-
fixion on Calvary. Nothing now remains of
that great city but an obelisk. Once there
were many, but they have wandered far from

the temple of learning where they were placed five thousand years ago. One stands in Alexandria where it was placed before the palace of Cleopatra, one has journeyed to Central Park, New York, and another to London.

We spent a day wandering through the corridors of the Gizeh museum, where are gathered the antiquities of Egypt in bewildering profusion. There we saw mummies of Rameses II, the conqueror of the East, the builder of temples, the greatest king that ever ruled in Egypt. He was the Pharaoh who "hardened his heart" against the Israelites. His features which are well preserved are dignified and commanding. The aquiline nose and broad forhead indicate a man of great mental force and determination.

Here also is the mummy of Sethi II, the Pharaoh of the Exodus, the contemporary of Moses. How surprised he would be to learn that his kingdom and his people have passed away, and the spokesman of that band of Jewish slaves became the spokesman of God to a large part of the world; and that the Jews are still a distinct people and are remarkably prosperous.

Old as Pharaoh is, he seems modern when

"Yankee Doodle" and the Statue of Rameses at Memphis.

compared to the wooden statue standing guard nearby. This statue is six thousand years old, two thousand years older than Pharaoh and Moses, and the wood is still well preserved. He is not at all Egyptian in appearance. It might be the likeness of a modern bonvivant or clubman. He has a jolly round face with a humorous, half-repressed smile. The Philosopher listening back six thousand years said he distinctly heard him laugh and remark, "That mother-in-law joke is a good one, but here is a conundrum given me by old Cheops who has that pyramid job down Memphis way, 'Why does a hen cross the road?'"

CHAPTER XLV.

HOMEWARD BOUND.

There comes a time in the course of travel when one has seen enough; when the sight of a temple, or a museum, or an art gallery brings no thrill of joy; when the brain is tired and overcrowded with scenes and incidents too rapidly accumulated to be properly filed away in the index of memory. Then is the time to rest,—then the time to remember the motto of the monkeys of Nikko, "See not too much, hear not too much, speak not too much."

Once more we went to the citadel to see the sun set across the valley of the Nile. Once more, and this time by moonlight, we contemplated the Pyramids, and watched their triangular shadows lengthen on the desert. Once more we bent our inquiring gaze upon the sad, mysterious face of the Sphinx before we could say farewell to Egypt, and farewell to the purple Orient and its strange people in the multi-colored clothing; for when we should reach Europe we would again be among the people of our occidental civilization.

As we completed the circuit of the world by sailing up New York harbor, Phil, the Philosopher from Philadelphia, gazed long and lovingly upon the "Gateway to America," and remarked, "After all, the best thing we have seen is the Statue of Liberty."

THE END.

EXTRACTS

FROM

HINDU LAL.

A New Book in Preparation

BY

DR. G. W. CALDWELL.

CHAPTER XII.

THE BROTHERHOOD OF THE VOLCANO.

We were well satisfied, the Professor and I, with our botanizing tour. With our little caravan of Gourka hill men and native ponies we had wandered over the ranges of the Himalayas studying and classifying the strange Flora with which the region abounds, and had finally arrived near the boundaries of the "Forbidden Land."

We were passing, that morning, up a wild ravine where jungle grass and stunted shrubs grew thick, and lichens clung to the rocky banks. Before us towered the mighty mountain—Jomo Kang Kar—"Our Lady of Snows," where the Gods and Goddesses of the Hindu mythology sit on their crystal thrones secure from mortal curiosity. Between us and the peak, which has never been scaled by man, lay snow fields broad and deep, sending down their glaciers to glitter pale blue in the sunlight, and melt into torrents which falling in feathery foam thousands of feet over the cliffs formed the river which rushed past us to join with the sacred Ganges on the plains of Hindustan.

In our travels we had learned from Ram Zan, our interpreter and guide, many secrets of the healing art unknown to the world outside of the hills of India, and, as said before, we were well satisfied with the benefit that the sick and suffering would receive when we should return to civilization and make them known.

Ram Zan was relating the strange stories of the Mahatmas, Yogis, Magi and Monks that have their habitations far in the wilds of these almost inaccessible mountains.

"This path," he said, "is worn by the pilgrims who travel to the Monastery of the Volcano to be healed by Swaami, the Holy Man, whose fame is as broad as India.

At that moment a cry was heard—the cry for aid of a man in terror. We seized our rifles and bidding our bearers follow, hurried up the ravine, answering the call. We had not traveled far when we saw crouching on a rock at the side of the ravine a tiger and a tigress. We three fired at the same moment, and the beasts sprang from the rock. One remained where he fell, but the tigress with a series of bounds crashed through the bushes and disappeared.

"Here is the pretty pussy," said the Professor, when we reached our trophy. "We must now learn whether the proprietor of the cry is inside," but we were saved the trouble, for only a few feet away we found the man among the rocks where he had fallen. He wore the robes of a priest of the higher order. He was badly injured, having fallen from the rocks and dislocated a hip and received a severe scalp wound from which the blood was still flowing.

We stripped his blood-stained turban into bandages, and by means of compresses and the icy waters, soon had the hemorrhage stopped and a neat bandage applied. Then we reduced the dislocation of the hip. The pain caused by such an injury and the manipulation of the bones is such as to bring groans of agony from the bravest man, but the priest calmly chewed some leaves which he picked out of the bag suspended from his shoulder. He showed no evidence of suffering.

Ram Zan noticed this and called our attention to the leaf which he recognized at once as a common umbelliferae. The priest admitted it was the "Pain Plant" of which we heard in Nepaul. At a later time we had an opportunity of putting this plant to the test in our own party, and found to our delight that it had the power of controlling pain without affecting consciousness.

In a short time the priest was strangely refreshed and strengthened. Through our interpreter he said:

"I thank you, Sahibs. You have saved my life; I am your servant, Hindu Lal, of the Monastery of the Volcano. As you see I am unable to walk, and a wounded man is an easy prey for wild beasts. I ask you to take me to the Monastery to-night."

"But the Monastery," we protested, "is two days' travel over the mountain."

"We will go by the secret passage," he replied. "In four hours we will reach the

Monastery. Swaami will not forget your
service, and if you seek knowledge, as I believe you do, since you were quick to detect
the Pain Plant, you shall learn of the master
what no man of your race has ever learned
before."

It was plain we could not leave him there
alone, so we placed him on a pony and proceeded up the path perhaps a half mile, when at his
direction we turned into a defile. As we proceeded the defile narrowed to a cleft in the
mountain, then abruptly terminated. Apparently we were in a pocket, and the only escape
was to return, but Hindu Lal bade us proceed to the extreme end of the cleft where the
vines climbed thickly up the rocks. The
vines proved to be only a curtain hiding the
entrance to a cave. Inside of the cave were
two hideous idols, with eyes of blood-red
carnelian, in the posture of forbidding entrance.

Our Gourka bearers were plainly frightened. Only after long persuasion was the
priest able to overcome their superstition.
Apparently the figures served well the purpose for which they were designed. Still
they reasoned that if it was safe to enter the
cave at all, it had better be done with a full

stomach, and they insisted on a halt for food.

At this the priest demurred. He wished
to proceed at once and as rapidly as possible,
so again he searched his bag and brought
forth another plant with a thick, glossy green
leaf, and calling to the men in the native
tongue, gave each a leaf and bade them eat.
The faith of the Gourkas in the priest was
remarkable. Each did as he was bidden.
We also received a portion and ate it. It
was strangely satisfying and seemed to ban-
ish fatigue and hunger like the cocoa leaves
which are chewed by the Indians of Peru.

The Gourkas were now willing to proceed.
We lighted torches which were found behind
the idols and entered the cave. We passed
along the lofty cavern between rows of idols
that glared at us with blood-red eyes. Our
voices echoed and re-echoed until they died
away in a faint call from the recesses of distant chambers.

At length we emerged from the cavern into
a circular valley surrounded by vertical cliffs,
inaccessible except at one point where a pathway zigzagged up to the crest.

"We have come through the secret passage," said Hindu Lal. "This valley is the
crater of an extinct volcano. The cloud of

steam arising yonder is from the natural hot springs, and nearby is the temple with the two colossal stone elephants before it."

As we passed down an avenue we saw many strange people camped in the shade of the banyan trees. They were pilgrims from all parts of India, who had come to be cured at the shrine of Swaami, the Holy Man of the Himalayas.

We halted at the gateway of the Monastery. Two attendants prostrated themselves before the priest, then tenderly lifted him from the horse and carried him in. We followed through an outer court brilliant with scarlet orchids,—through stone corridors, the walls of which were covered with astrological and mystical signs,—across a curious inner court, in the pavement of which a brazen sun was inset, surrounded by the elliptic, the signs of the Zodiac, and other emblems which we did not understand. A door mysteriously opened and closed for us. Our feet sank into the deep, rich pile of oriental rugs. The air became heavy with the odors of burning incense. A moment later we stood in the presence of Swaami, the Holy Man.

He sat on a cushion, with his legs folded

as a woman folds her arms. He was thin to
emaciation and for clothes he wore only a
loin cloth of pure white silk. Unlike other
holy men of India we had seen, he was clean
—scrupulously clean. His face was strong,
and kind, and in his eye was wisdom and con-
scious power.

Behind the Holy Man stood an idol of
terrifying aspect. Its eyes were blazing
rubies and an enormous diamond scintillated
on its forehead. The interior of its wide-
open mouth was blood-red, and for teeth it
had rows of jagged quartz crystals. Over
its shoulder was a cape of human vertebrae,
with a fringe of finger bones, and with a skull
as a central pendant.

Hindu Lal narrated the story of his misfortune and our timely rescue. At its end
Swaami smiled upon us, and placing his left
hand over his heart, touched his lips and forehead with the fingers of his right hand, which
we learned was the secret sign of the Brotherhood.

Attendants removed the bandages from
Hindu Lal, and after washing the wound, applied some aromatic balm. A tiny glass of
red liquid was given him and in a few minutes his weakness disappeared.

"By your kindness to me," he said, "you have won what no man of your race could buy. It is the wish of The Master that you be shown the mysteries of healing, which throughout all ages have been reserved for the elect of the Brotherhood."

A pilgrim was brought in, leaning heavily upon the arm of an attendant. His breath came fast and short and from his chest issued wheezing sounds. "Save me, oh Master, else I die. A demon is in my chest and he grapples at my throat. Drive him out, oh Master," he panted as he prostrated himself before the Holy Man.

"Behold the herb the Master will give him," whispered Hindu Lal. "Note the round leaves and the purple veins. To it is given dominion over the Fiend of the Air. With it will the Master exorcise the demon and he shall trouble him no more. One leaf shall he eat at the rising of the sun and the going down thereof for the space of three moon cycles and he shall trouble the man no more."

The pilgrim took from his finger a jeweled ring and placing it in the palm of the idol, passed out.

Then came a man from Thibet, being carried in a chair. "Oh Master," he said, "the

wrath of the Gods rest heavily upon me.   I
can neither lift my right foot or my right
hand."

. "By this," said Hindu Lal, "will the spell
be broken.   By this will be he healed.   It is
the Spirit Plant.   Place your fingers upon it."
We did so and received a sensation similar to
an electric shock.

"He who gathers it," continued the priest,
"must needs be cautious.   It was that which
caused my fall from the cliff this morning
when you rescued me.   At the magic hour
must it be gathered, for only then is the spirit
upon it."

He gave some leaves to the paralytic, and
when he had eaten he clapped his hands for
joy, and descending from his chair, took a
heavy gold chain from his neck and placing
it in the palm of the idol, went out praising,
strange as it may seem, not the Holy Man or
the remedy, but the idol.

"These poor people," said the Master,
"must have a fetish.   With their eyes must
they see a physical object, for their minds
are not capable of comprehending the invisible.   Therefore do they bring their jewels
and offer them to the idol, and it is well, for
therewith may the brothers buy rice, and the

wise men spend their days in study of the mysteries of Nature for the benefit of the people."

"In this," he continued, showing us a red liquid, "are the elements of life, and it is capable of saving those suffering from disease as bread saves those starving for food. With these elements Nature makes her repairs. My sons, in these mountains human life on this planet began, and in these secluded monasteries are secrets of Nature kept until the world shall be ready to receive them. They will be revealed to you when you shall become one of us, and shall have taken the oath of the Brotherhood before the blood-red eye of Zarlon the All-Seeing. The ordeal is prepared. The brothers await you in the Cavern of the Eternal Fire."

www.ingramcontent.com/pod-product-compliance
Lightning Source LLC
La Vergne TN
LVHW051252080426
835509LV00020B/2940